MW01119440

Boiled Beans
on Toast

Also by Girish Karnad

Tughlaq
Hayavadana
Naga-Mandala
The Fire and the Rain
The Dreams of Tipu Sultan & Bali: The Sacrifice
Yayati
Wedding Album

THREE PLAYS
[*Tughlaq* • *Hayavadana* • *Naga-Mandala*]

COLLECTED PLAYS, VOL. I
[*Tughlaq* • *Hayavadana* • *Bali: The Sacrifice* • *Naga-Mandala*]

COLLECTED PLAYS, VOL. II
[*Taledanda* • *The Fire and the Rain* • *The Dreams of Tipu Sultan* •
Two Dramatic Monologues: Flowers and Broken Images]

Girish Karnad

Boiled Beans
on Toast

A Play

HUMBER LIBRARIES LAKESHORE CAMPUS
3199 Lakeshore Blvd West
TORONTO, ON. M8V 1K8

OXFORD
UNIVERSITY PRESS

OXFORD
UNIVERSITY PRESS

Oxford University Press is a department of the University of Oxford.
It furthers the University's objective of excellence in research, scholarship,
and education by publishing worldwide. Oxford is a registered trademark of
Oxford University Press in the UK and in certain other countries

Published in India by
Oxford University Press
YMCA Library Building, 1 Jai Singh Road, New Delhi 110 001, India

© Oxford University Press 2014

The moral rights of the author have been asserted

First Edition published in 2014

All rights reserved. No part of this publication may be reproduced, stored in
a retrieval system, or transmitted, in any form or by any means, without the
prior permission in writing of Oxford University Press, or as expressly permitted
by law, by licence, or under terms agreed with the appropriate reprographics
rights organization. Enquiries concerning reproduction outside the scope of the
above should be sent to the Rights Department, Oxford University Press, at the
address above

You must not circulate this work in any other form
and you must impose this same condition on any acquirer

ISBN-13: 978-0-19-809860-7
ISBN-10: 0-19-809860-X

Typeset in 10.5/14 Minion Pro
by Excellent Laser Typesetters, Pitampura, Delhi 110 034
Printed in India by Akash Press, New Delhi 110 020

For Madeline Pouzo
with affection, admiration, and thanks

A Note on the Title

The title of the play relates to the founding myth of the city of Bengaluru or Bangalore, which is today admired as the 'Silicon Valley of India' and is the subject of this play.

In the eleventh century, King Veera Ballala went out hunting, lost his way in the jungle, and after wandering through the night, arrived exhausted at a lonely hut where an old woman saved his life by giving him a handful of boiled beans (*benda kaalu* in Kannada, the native tongue). In gratitude, the King named the place 'BendaKaaluru', the place of boiled beans, which in the course of time got corrupted into 'Bengaluru' and was in turn anglicized by the colonial rulers into 'Bangalore'.

The toast is a strictly Western import into Indian cuisine.

The Kannada title of the play is *Benda Kaalu on Toast*.

Foreword

The chief protagonist of *Boiled Beans on Toast* is the city of Bangalore, a throbbing organism spawned by globalization. The play holds a mirror to the fractured lives of its floating population which occupies a broad social spectrum from the struggler to the street-smart survivor, from the small-town aspirant to the elite. This is a city of wild hopes and dashed dreams, of disappointment and despair, of environmental destruction and rapid development.

Anjana Padabidri, the central character, weeps over the axing down of the magnificent rain tree across the road—a tree because of which she built her house there. Her friend Dolly, a high-society battered wife with little to occupy her, rues the cement concrete that is replacing trees everywhere. However, what she rues, Prabhakar Telang finds exciting. He has never seen tall, glass-fronted buildings except on television, in the small town in the Western Ghats from where he comes. For him they spell promise. For Vimla, the family servant on the make, the anonymity that the city offers, provides convenient cover.

Karnad observes these characters with a sense of irony, maintaining a remarkably objective viewpoint devoid of nostalgia. The play is neither loaded with memories of a golden past, nor does it take a moralistic stand against development. It looks at the reality of the present with unblinking eyes. The only time Karnad allows himself to judge is at the end, when Anjana's musician son, Kunal, describes Bangalore as a 'Big Black Hole'.

Although one might with reason label the play realistic, chiefly because its characters are drawn with great attention to socio-psychological truth, the play departs enough from the conventionally realistic play in structure and purpose for the label to come unstuck. The realistic play belongs to a time when narratives could be woven around a single focus, allowing a sedate development from exposition to complication to resolution. *Boiled Beans on Toast* belongs to a world of multiple misalignments. If its purpose is to encompass the heterogeneity of the lives and dreams that make the organism tick, it has no choice but to discard linearity and the idea of a satisfying resolution.

Structurally, *Boiled Beans on Toast* works as a prose symphony, the dominant theme being configured through long and short movements. The opening altercation between Muttu and her brother might then be regarded as the overture, introducing aspects of the theme to be explored—village versus city; human relations guided by family and community ties versus human relations guided by pragmatic principles; the idea of home, ancestral versus self-made. Like much modern music, here too there are more dissonant than consonant notes.

Boiled Beans on Toast had its premiere in a widely appreciated Marathi production in Pune in February 2013. Adapted by Pradeep Vaiddya and directed by Mohit Takalkar for the theatre company Aasakta, *Uney Pure Shahar Ek* (One City, More or Less) transposed the play from Bangalore to Pune. The fit was perfect, for Pune has followed a graph of growth similar to Bangalore's, progressing from an old, leafy university town to an overcrowded city dominated by information technology and the service industry.

29 June 2013   SHANTA GOKHALE
Mumbai

BOILED BEANS ON TOAST

Boiled Beans on Toast was first presented in a Marathi adaptation titled, *Uney Purey Shahar Ek*, at the Yashwantrao Chavan Natyagruha, Pune, by the Aasakta group on 1 March 2013. It was sponsored by the Sahitya Rangabhoomi Pratisthan. The principal cast was as follows, although the names of some characters differed in the Marathi version:

ANITA DATE	Muttu
RADHIKA APTE	Vimala
PRATIBHA DATE	Muttu's mother
UMESH JAGTAP	Shankara / Sundara Rajan
ASHWINI GIRI	Anjana
VIBHAWARI DESHPANDE	Dolly Iyer
SAGAR DESHMUKH	Prabhakar
JYOTI SUBHASH	Anusuya
SIDDHARTH MENON	Kunaal
RAVI SANGVAI	Brigadier Iyer
PRAJAKTA SALBARDE	Sumitra
DEVENDRA GAIKWAD	Inspector / Ravi
PRAJAKTA PATIL	Saroja
RAHUL PARKHE	Head Constable
SHEKH MADAM	Lady Constable
LAXMI BIRAJDAR	Vimala's sister-in-law / Shankara's wife
VEERA SAXENA	Receptionist
RAHUL PARBHE	'Wipro' guard
SAYALI DEVDHAR	
PRAJAKTA SALBARDE	
VRUSHALI DUBEY	Village women
PRAJAKTA PATIL	
SWAMINI DUBEY	

Directed by	MOHIT TAKALKAR
Set design by	MOHIT TAKALKAR
Lighting design by	PRADEEP VAIDDYA
Translated by	PRADEEP VAIDDYA
Sound design by	DARSHAN PATANKAR
Costumes by	RASHMI RODE

Act One

Scene One

As the lights come on, the entire cast is seen on stage in a phantasma-goric tableau, every character immobile, frozen in the middle of some activity. When the lights are fully on, the actors spring into action, talking, moving about, fighting, shouting, bumping into each other, the background noise of traffic and music adding to the effect of a busy thoroughfare in Bangalore. Then the lights and the music fade out together.

Scene Two

Anjana Padabidri's house. Muttu, the maid, aged about twenty-eight, is ironing clothes in the service room. Vimala, the cook and the chief servant of the house, aged thirty-five, enters accompanied by Muttu's mother and elder brother, Shankara. The mother leans heavily on a triple-hoofed stick as she walks.

VIMALA: Muttu, visitors for you.

MUTTU: Oh god! Why have you come in here? You know Amma—

VIMALA (*to the mother*): You know the rules perfectly well. Amma doesn't like all this crowding in and holding your family conferences here. Muttu's been given a mobile and you know what that's for.

MOTHER: Shankara arrived all of a sudden from our town. He says he has to go back by this evening.

VIMALA: If you'd called Muttu on the mobile, she would've come out for a while. There's no need for you to storm into the house like an army. Please don't do it again.
(*Goes out.*)

SHANKARA: Goodness me! Who's that?

MUTTU: Vimala, the cook. She's been here for ever and she thinks she's the mistress of the house.

SHANKARA (*inspects the house*): A nice big house, I must say.

MUTTU: But she's right. You shouldn't have just come in like this. It annoys Amma. You know that, Mother. We could've met at home in the evening. Or if you'd called me, I would've come out.

SHANKARA: I don't have till the evening. The moment he received his call from Bengaluru, the Boss said let's go and we started immediately. He's been nice enough to let me take the car to meet you while he's at his meeting. I've only got a couple of hours here and then I've to drive him back. Then I had to pick up Mother on the way.

MOTHER: I said I won't come. But he wouldn't listen.

SHANKARA: If I knew where this house was, I wouldn't have troubled you, Mother. Do you think I've nothing else to do but hound you? Besides, I needed you here. There's something very important I've to discuss with you both. I'll do that and leave.

MUTTU (*guardedly*): You could've called me on the mobile.

SHANKARA (*annoyed*): There are things you can't talk about on the phone. Don't you understand? It's a family matter. Don't worry, I won't stay long. Now, I got your letter saying Kalpana's come of age. And you say you want to have all the rituals done here in Bengaluru. Why? Isn't it a matter of happiness for us that your daughter's matured? Who do we have here in this city? All our relations live in Karimangala or Solagiri. They can't come this far for the ceremony.

MUTTU: Husband said Karimangala would mean expense. The remotest relatives'll turn up. In Bengaluru, we can have a smaller affair. More compact.

SHANKARA (*to the mother*): And you agreed?

MOTHER: It's their daughter. Who am I to advise? But what her husband says makes sense. What's the point of spending unnecessarily?

SHANKARA: That's what happens when people move to the city. The family back home, relatives, connections—they all become dispensable, don't they? They can be put aside. Ignored. Forgotten.

MUTTU: I don't know what to say. You talk to Husband.

SHANKARA: I don't have time now to go searching for Brother-in-law. His factory's beyond the old airport, miles away. Now listen to me. Don't I feel happy if my sister's only daughter comes of age? Should we not celebrate it in our ancestral home in our own town? I refuse to come to Bengaluru with my family for a meal as though I was attending a function in some stranger's house. You and I—we grew up in Karimangala. Our family gods are there. I insist that we celebrate this event in our own house. If you're afraid of the expense, I'll handle it myself.

MUTTU: Husband'll look after all that.

SHANKARA: Leave the money matters to the men. I'll convince him. Let Kalpana finish her exams. There's no hurry. There're only three girls in our family, after all. You have one and I've two. Kalpana is the eldest of the three. Let's invite all the family members— elders, cousins, aunts, uncles—and perform the rites properly.
(*Muttu looks at the mother.*)

MOTHER: As the men decide. What can I say?
(*Vimala enters, looking busy.*)

VIMALA: Have you finished, Muttu?

MUTTU: Yes, yes. Only two pieces left.

VIMALA: When're you going to be done? This is why Amma forbids these family sessions here. Then the grandmother's here from Dharwad. And the old lady needs attention hand and foot. Get on with it.

SHANKARA: All right, all right, we're done. It was just a very important family issue. We won't bother you again, I promise you. Or else next time I shall have the siren on, warning you of our arrival, like in an ambulance.

MUTTU: Brother, please—

Shankara: Or even better, I'll make sure you're not in town when we come. All right? Let's go, Mother.

(*Shankara and the mother leave. Vimala's voice is loud enough to ensure that he hears her comment.*)

VIMALA: Is that your brother? I should ask him to learn a little civility. This isn't your backwoods, you know. This is Bengaluru. We can do with less rudeness here.

(*Goes out. Muttu continues with her ironing.*)

Scene Three

The living room of the Padabidri house. Anjana and her friend, Dolly. Anjana is in her mid-forties while Dolly is in her late-thirties. Vimala is pouring tea into the cups on the table and laying out biscuits and sandwiches. Intermittently, one can hear Kunaal practising on his guitar in his room.

ANJANA: ... And slowly, you know, you begin to realize that the flip side of life isn't death—it's pain. When they're in pain, the patients can't think of anything else. It fills every crack in their consciousness. It blanks everything out, blinds them, deafens them to the world. But when they're given palliatives and the pain begins to recede—my god! The change! Their interest in life revives. They become human. They begin to discuss their problems with you. Their hopes, plans. It's wonderful!

DOLLY (*to Vimala*): Only one spoon, please.

VIMALA: I know.

DOLLY: But Anjana, they are brought to the Karunashraya and it's only *then* that they know there's no going back? How terrible!

ANJANA: Not always. Sometimes the families tell them what it means. But often they don't. They pretend they're being taken to a new hospital, to another specialist. It can be awful, I agree.

DOLLY: But when they realize they've been brought under false pretences, don't they feel cheated? Throw a fit?
(*The doorbell rings. Anjana calls out.*)

ANJANA: Muttu—

VIMALA: I'll attend to it. Muttu must be cleaning the Master's study. (*Vimala goes out.*)

DOLLY: That must be awful. To come in the hope of being cured and then find there's no going back. The very thought gives me the shivers—

ANJANA: They do get upset. But the funny thing is, often, when the truth sinks in, the patients feel the family was right not to tell them. 'I would've done the same,' they say. Almost grateful that the lie kept hope alive for that much longer, you know.

DOLLY: But, Anjana, to tell a person that she's going to die—

ANJANA (*smiles*): No, no, no. However terminal the cancer, you never say to a patient, 'You're going to die.' You just say, 'I'm sorry but we won't be able to cure you.' You see, you never know. The patient may not die. There are cases we thought hopeless, still alive.

VIMALA (*enters*): Someone to see the Master. He's given his card.

ANJANA: But Mr Padabidri isn't in Bangalore today. Didn't you tell him? Anyway why's this man here? He should go to the office.
(*Puts the visiting card down on the table without even looking at it.*)
VIMALA: I told him. But he says he was specifically asked to come to the house. Not the office.

ANJANA: How annoying!

VIMALA: There he is.
(*Prabhakar enters. He is about thirty-five, dressed in a cheap suit and a tie. He is sweating profusely. Vimala casts an annoyed look at him for entering so unceremoniously and goes in. He doesn't know which of the two women is Mrs Padabidri.*)

PRABHAKAR: Good morning. My name is Prabhakar Telang. Mr Padabidri had asked me to meet him here this morning.

ANJANA: I'm sorry, but my husband isn't back in town.

PRABHAKAR: Oh but—but he gave me an appointment—for this morning.

ANJANA: I know. I know. He should've been back from Canada two days ago. But he was instructed by his office to go on to Finland. Didn't his secretary inform you?

PRABHAKAR: Actually his secretary doesn't know about this meeting. This was arranged independently. (*Pause. Almost conspiratorially*) By a mutual acquaintance.
(*He is perspiring profusely. Wipes his face.*)

ANJANA: Please sit down. Would you like some tea?

PRABHAKAR: No, no, thanks. (*Pause.*) I don't want to trouble you.

ANJANA: No trouble at all. (*Calls out.*) Vimala, another cup of tea, please.

PRABHAKAR: Thank you. You see, I've come all the way from K.R. Puram in a rickshaw. It took nearly an hour and a half. Actually I'm very late for the appointment. Mr Padabidri would be right to be upset. But the traffic's unbelievable. We were stationary most of the time.

ANJANA: I'm Anjana, Mrs Padabidri. This is Mrs Dolly Iyer, a family friend. I'm afraid my husband may not be back for another four or five days. May be even longer.

PRABHAKAR: Oh, dear! That would be—a huge problem.

ANJANA: I'm sorry. Was it something urgent?
(*Vimala comes in with another cup of tea and a teapot and a bowl of sugar.*)

VIMALA (*to Dolly*): You haven't touched your tea, Madam. It'll have gone cold by now. I'll get you some fresh tea.

DOLLY: No, no, please don't worry.

VIMALA: It's no bother. You like your tea boiling hot, I know that. (*Picks up the tray which she had brought earlier.*)

ANJANA (*to Prabhakar*): Please, have your tea.

PRABHAKAR: Yes, I shall, if you don't mind. Otherwise my tea'll get cold by the time yours comes back and then you'll have to wait while my tea is taken away and heated up again. And so on. (*They all laugh.*)

ANJANA: I'm sorry but I can't understand why my husband should call you home. Most unusual.

PRABHAKAR: It's about a vacancy in his office.

ANJANA: Really? But he moved out of Administration some time ago. He's in Finance Management now.

PRABHAKAR: No, no, let me—let me explain properly. I've a temporary position in my office. I'm on probation. But the prospects are good. The point is—it's a confidential matter.

ANJANA: Then you don't need to talk about it.

PRABHAKAR: No, no. It's not like that. You are, after all, Mrs Padabidri, so I'm sure Mr Padabidri hides nothing from you. And she's your family friend. So—

ANJANA (*smiles*): Relax, Mr Telang. As I said, you don't have to tell us—
(*Anjana and Dolly look at each other and smile, which he notices. It confuses him even more.*)

PRABHAKAR (*anguished*): Please, please, don't misunderstand me. That's not what I meant. The fact is—the boss of the company in which I'm at present employed, is going to quit and join Mr Padabidri's office—and he's taking four of our top-notch managers along with him. His favourites. It's all rather hush hush, as you can imagine. I'm not one of them—yet—but there's a chance I may be taken up along with them.

DOLLY: Oh, congratulations.

PRABHAKAR: But Mr Padabidri's never met me. It's only my boss's recommendation. So he—that is, Mr Padabidri—has asked me to come here and meet him, so we could discuss the situation over a cup of tea. Well, I've got my cup of tea, but I haven't met him.

(*They all laugh. Vimala brings a fresh tray with two cups and places it on the table. She looks around to see if anything more is required.*)

PRABHAKAR (*covering his cup with his palm rather dramatically*): Mine is hot. Piping.

(*They laugh. Vimala is not particularly amused at this familiarity and goes in. A long pause.*)

PRABHAKAR (*almost to himself*): The problem is another four or five days means the news will be out, there'll be pandemonium in our office, I don't know what'll happen then. Anything could. They could target me and terminate my services. That would be the end of my hopes, that's for certain.

ANJANA: I'm sorry to hear that. That's very thoughtless of my husband. (*Pause. They have run out of conversation. But he hasn't finished his tea yet.*)

PRABHAKAR: The road outside your house is like a scene from a war movie.

ANJANA: They're building an underpass there, so they are chopping down the trees.

DOLLY: The problem is our City Corporation is run by people born and brought up in the countryside. They've no time for greenery and environment. They simply love cement concrete, and plastic and glass-fronted buildings. That means modernity to them.

PRABHAKAR: Like me, you mean? But then, you see, you can't blame them. A city is meant for people, so that they can live there. Believe in its solidity. Madam, I grew up in the heart of the

Western Ghats—the thickest of forests—near Mundgod—and I grew up yearning for the massive constructions of cement concrete and the towering glass-fronted skyscrapers I saw on television.

ANJANA: You know the main reason for this house being here is that tree outside. Kunaal and I were scouting around Bangalore for a suitable area in which to build our house—that was of course more than fifteen years ago—it was still possible to buy a plot of land you liked on which you might want to build your house—

DOLLY: Ah, for those days, Anjana! Land? You would be lucky to find an apartment today.

ANJANA: We saw this magnificent tree along the wide road—you know with its foliage spreading like an umbrella—and I said to Kunaal, 'Look, Kunaal, that is a rain tree. It has bipinnate leaves—like feathers—they open up in the sun so you've shade under it during the day and they fold in at night, so moonlight filters through.' He was absolutely delighted and we immediately decided to build our house there. We planned the whole layout, standing right there, so that the terrace would be under its spreading branches, and we could have regular dinner parties on it.

PRABHAKAR: You only have to dream of something and you can turn it into a reality. How marvellous!

ANJANA: But of course the City Corporation has other ideas now. They've joined the wide road in front to the Mysore arterial highway and turned it into a ring road. That was the end of our dinner parties. The traffic was deafening. You couldn't hear a word of what the next person said. Now they say the ring road gets choked up, so they've to have an underpass and the trees have to go. There's talk now of widening the road to a hundred and fifty feet! There's simply no end. Kunaal and I—we love that rain tree, and I swear to you the day that tree goes I'm getting out of this house.

DOLLY: My husband was posted here in Bangalore when he was in service and fondly remembered the Cantonment bungalows. The pillars, the porticos, and the monkeytop windows. We come here now and bungalows! Ha! (*Throws up hands dramatically.*) We decided to settle for a comfortable apartment.

PRABHAKAR: Comfortable! Lucky you, Madam! You should see our flat. It's the size of a handkerchief. But then, you see, who asked me to come to Bengaluru? Who asked anyone to come to Bengaluru? With people pouring into the city—

(*Vimala enters.*)

VIMALA: Time for your pills, Amma. I've kept them next to the saucers. I'll find out if Grandma needs anything before she goes out.

(*Goes in.*)

DOLLY: Anjana, I'm willing to put up with the tiniest of apartments, if only I could find someone like your Vimala to run the house. Where did you find her?

ANJANA: We were building this house and she simply turned up and asked if she could work here. I needed a cook desperately and that was it.

PRABHAKAR: And you took her on as a cook without worrying about her caste, customs—

ANJANA: Mr Telang, let me put in a word of caution. If you are going to work for my husband, you would be well advised not to speak of caste and community.

PRABHAKAR (*jumping up*): Oh, Madam, I don't believe in caste at all. I consider myself a secular, leftwing intellectual—

(*Anjana's mobile rings. She checks the caller's name.*)

ANJANA: Excuse me.

(*The guitar music ends on a high note.*)

PRABHAKAR (*embarrassed at his own gaucherie*): That was nice music.

ANJANA (*as she hurries in*): Thanks. My son Kunaal.

PRABHAKAR: I don't understand Western music. But that music's nice. (*Anjana disappears into the house.*)

DOLLY (*lowering her voice*): Listen, Mr Telang, I want to tell you something. Something important. It could help you with your career.

PRABHAKAR (*startled*): My career? What?

DOLLY (*picking up his visiting card from the table*): We can't talk about it here. Let's meet somewhere else. In the next day or two. You know the Café Coffee Day near the Ashoka Pillar? Good. I'll give you a ring on your mobile. (*Looks at her watch.*) Where's my husband? We can't afford to be late for lunch. We are meant to be lunching with Kiran Mazumdar and John Shaw—you know, the Managing Director of the Biocon Empire. They are dear friends.

(*Anusuya, a gracious old lady in her seventies, enters, followed by Vimala carrying her bag which bulges with her needs. Prabhakar stands up.*)

VIMALA: I'll keep this bag in the car, Grandma. (*Goes out.*)

DOLLY: How are you, Auntie? How was the train trip?

ANUSUYA: What can I say? They always allot me an upper berth in the sleeper. And my age is printed, right there on the ticket.
(*They laugh.*)

DOLLY: I presume they changed it.

ANUSUYA: The conductor insisted he had no spare sleepers until I threatened to spread my sheet out, right there, in the corridor and go to sleep on the floor. That always works.
(*More laughter.*)

DOLLY: And what's the itinerary today? Visiting some temple?

ANUSUYA: No, thanks. My official quota for temples has been long met. Some shopping, probably. Don't know what. All the shops seem to sell the same things. (*Pointing to Anjana*) And she, of course, isn't in the least interested. Busy with her hospice.

DOLLY: But have you seen the hospice building, Auntie? You should. It's so beautifully designed, so tranquil—

ANUSUYA: There was something in the papers today about the race course. It said they're going to close it down and move it out of the city.

DOLLY: It's simple, Auntie. The Chief Minister has his eyes on all that open space in the heart of the city. A gold mine.

ANUSUYA: I've never been to a horse race and if I'm not going to get another chance, I might as well peep in.
(*Anjana enters, obviously upset.*)

ANJANA: Was there anything else, Mr Telang?

PRABHAKAR: No, not at all, Madam. I was just waiting to say thank you and bid goodbye.

ANJANA: I'll tell my husband you were here.

PRABHAKAR: Please. And thank you, Mrs Iyer.
(*Dolly and Prabhakar exchange quick looks and he goes out. Kunaal enters with his guitar in its bag. He is in his late teens.*)

ANUSUYA: Are you keeping me company, Kunu?

KUNAAL: I've arranged an escort for you. A Mr Sundara Rajan. He's the official man-for-all-seasons—looks after their visitors.

ANUSUYA: Thanks. I'll be back soon, Anjana.

ANJANA: Take your time.

KUNAAL: Have fun, Grandma. Mummy, if it gets very late, I may not come home for dinner. I'll sleep over at Nandita's.

ANUSUYA: Who's Nandita?

KUNAAL: The singer in our band. She's absolutely amazing.
(*Startled, Anusuya looks at Anjana, who doesn't show any reaction although she has registered Anusuya's sense of shock.*)

ANJANA: If I'm not going to see you before tomorrow morning, I want to have a word with you. Papa called.
(*Kunaal groans. Anusuya senses the tension in the air.*)

ANUSUYA: I'll be off then.

ANJANA and DOLLY: Bye.
(*Anusuya goes out by the front door.*)

KUNAAL: I've a rehearsal, Mummy. They'll be waiting.

DOLLY (*anticipating trouble*): I'd better go. My husband's probably stuck somewhere. His mobile's busy too.
(*Anjana nods. Muttu comes out running holding a thermos flask.*)

MUTTU: Amma, Grandma's forgotten her thermos flask.

ANJANA: Why're you telling me? Run out and give it to Grandma before she drives off.
(*Muttu runs out.*)

DOLLY: Needs to be told everything, doesn't she?

ANJANA: A good girl. A bit slow though.

DOLLY: Well, you can't expect to find a Vimala every time.
(*Anjana smiles absent-mindedly and nods.*)

I shouldn't have recommended a visit to the hospice to the old lady, should I? She didn't seem to like it.

ANJANA: I don't think she minded.
(*Dolly waves to Kunaal and goes out. Pause.*)

KUNAAL (*defiant*): Yes, Mummy. Papa called. So?

ANJANA: He's seen the credit card statement. You have bought a new, expensive guitar.

KUNAAL: Not expensive. Just a good one. Actually, I need a better one—a resonator—and was tempted by a Dobro. But resisted.

ANJANA: How are you going to make a living playing the guitar? What kind of future—

KUNAAL: Please let's not go over that again. I know every argument. I've to have a guitar. And I need it now, while I'm struggling to make a name for myself. *Not* when I'm bent and old and thirty-five.

ANJANA: I wish you and your father would decide between yourselves.

KUNAAL: But surely that's not what Papa called for. I want to be a musician and I hope Papa will support me till I can afford to be on my own. He knows that.

ANJANA: I think half his worries would be over if you just passed your exams.

KUNAAL (*exasperated*): Mummy, why did he call?

ANJANA: He's received an anonymous letter saying—your drummer is gay.

KUNAAL: I can't believe it! Perhaps he is. Perhaps he is a transsexual. What am I supposed to do about it? He drums like a god.

ANJANA: And that the pad or the club or whatever it is where you play has a reputation for rave parties and drugs.

KUNAAL: I'm going.
(*Starts walking out.*)

ANJANA: I wish you two would leave me out of it. I can't stand it any longer. All I can say is I'm glad his job keeps him away from India. It keeps me sane.

KUNAAL: And I shall also oblige by staying out tonight.
(*He walks out. Her mobile rings. She speaks into it.*)

ANJANA (*on the mobile*): So the ambulance was there on time. Good. I'll start right away.

Scene Four

The gallery of the Bangalore Race Course.

Later that day. Anusuya and Sundara Rajan are watching the end of a race. The soundtrack recreates the excited commotion as a race ends, and the commentator's voice describes the last section of the race and confirms the results. Anusuya is hopping mad.

ANUSUYA: I can't believe it! No Number Eight. No Five. Not even a place. Sundara Rajan, I said let's place a bet on Number Four. But you didn't listen. We lost a fluke win!

SUNDARA RAJAN: Madam, I said nothing. I merely—

ANUSUYA: Don't make excuses now. Didn't I specifically tell you to bet on Number Four? Four. We would have made a killing. But you had to—Did I or did I not ask you to bet on Four?

SUNDARA RAJAN: You did, Madam. But there's no money left. And you don't have a credit card. There was nothing to—

ANUSUYA: Now don't interfere with my instructions any more. Let's look at the next race. I'd actually marked—
(*Refers to her notebook.*)

SUNDARA RAJAN: Madam, we have no money left. We've lost the last rupee we brought.

ANUSUYA: No money? How's that possible? Why didn't we bring enough?

SUNDARA RAJAN: I was only supposed to take you round the city. I didn't know you—we—were going to bet on horses.

ANUSUYA: Nor did I, if that's any help. I didn't realize races were like this. That they gobble up money.

SUNDARA RAJAN: You've bet in every single race since we arrived, Madam.

ANUSUYA: And won. I won the very first race. And won places in two later ones. And then in the fifth race I actually made—

SUNDARA RAJAN: I know, Madam. And staked that amount back again. I told you we should place smaller bets. But you wouldn't listen.

ANUSUYA: Stop advising me. We must look for some more money. Isn't there anyone we could borrow from?

SUNDARA RAJAN: People come here to gamble. Not to lend money.

ANUSUYA: I know, I know. Couldn't you go out and borrow from that Ramayya Chetty shop? They were so nice and polite this morning.

SUNDARA RAJAN: I'll have to go out of the compound for that. And we'll miss the next one.

ANUSUYA: We can't. This's the last one for the day.

SUNDARA RAJAN: I know. Madam, let's just watch the race and go home.

ANUSUYA: But Silver Stallion! We simply—oh god!
(*Inspects the crowds with desperate intensity. Suddenly*)

Sundara Rajan, that man there. Rather stuffy-looking gentleman. In the grey suit. Who's he? Looks familiar.

SUNDARA RAJAN: That's the Brigadier. Husband of Dolly Iyer—you know, Mrs Padabidri's friend.

ANUSUYA: Of course that's him. Will you please call him? Quick. Say I want to talk to him.

(*Sundara Rajan goes to Brigadier Iyer and brings him to Anusuya.*)

SUNDARA RAJAN: Brigadier sir, this is Mrs Padabidri, my boss's mother. She wanted to—

BRIGADIER: Of course I know her. We've met at Anjana's. A couple of times, actually. (*To Anusuya*) As you know, my wife spends so much time in your house you could legitimately charge her rent.

(*Laughs.*) Are you on your own?

ANUSUYA: No, no. Sundara Rajan's there, as you can see. Brigadier, can I bother you for a favour?

BRIGADIER: But of course. What can I do for you?

ANUSUYA: Can I ask for a small loan? Only temporarily.

BRIGADIER (*startled*): A loan? But of course. Except that I don't carry much cash on me.

ANUSUYA: Oh! I don't need much. A few thousand? Ten?

(*The Brigadier, taken aback, fumbles through his pockets, takes out his wallet and starts checking the cash.*)

Even five'll do. You see, I have an excellent hunch for the next race. Not a hunch—a tip—a certain win. I shall return the loan the moment my horse wins.

BRIGADIER: But of course. The point is I hadn't come for the races. I've an appointment with Doctor Gowda, the Chairman of the Turf Club. Let me see how much I have. Hmm! Sorry but I've only four thousand on me.

ANUSUYA: That'll do. Thank you. It's better than nothing. And I shall return it the moment the race's over.

BRIGADIER: I shouldn't worry, Mrs Padabidri. There's absolutely no hurry. I can always get it back from Mr Padabidri or Anjana.

ANUSUYA: That's it, Brigadier. Please, please, please don't say anything to my son or daughter-in-law about it. I shall be most thankful if you mentioned absolutely nothing to them. I shall return the amount the moment the race's over. Now if you'll excuse me. Please, hurry. Sundara Rajan. Three thousand on Silver Stallion for a win. God, I'm excited! And yes, one for a place. Same horse.

(*The Brigadier watches bemused.*)

Scene Five

Café Coffee Day. Prabhakar is sitting at a table, immersed in a book. The alarm on his mobile rings. He looks up, sees Dolly arriving from a distance, and quickly shoves the book into his briefcase. And sits, his hands folded, watching the street, seemingly idly. When a bearer approaches him he waves him away as though to say, 'Later'. Dolly arrives.

DOLLY: Good morning. I hope I haven't kept you waiting.

PRABHAKAR: Not at all. Actually you're on time. I chose to be early. Because I love to sit and watch the traffic in the streets of Bangalore. I can sit like this for hours—transfixed.

DOLLY: Really? Most people grumble about our endless traffic.

PRABHAKAR: When I was young I was taken to Gokarn, to the beach. And I had never seen the sea before. I had grown up in the jungles and although the sea was less than fifty miles away, had no idea what it looked like. And I was mesmerized. Waves after waves after waves and then water, right up to the horizon. Our traffic too is like that. Waves after waves of scooters, autorickshaws, buses, cars, every conceivable kind of vehicle, including bullock carts, tractors, and earth movers. It's magical.

DOLLY: I must say you seemed such a scared little yokel when we met at Anjana's. You're a different person now.

PRABHAKAR: When you've grown up in a small town, these city bungalows have a strange effect on you. My entire body begins to shrink, you know. And the tongue refuses to turn the way I want it to. In such situations, I find it's safer to play the innocent fool—it's a safeguard against humiliation.

DOLLY: You're good with words. Do you write poetry?

PRABHAKAR: There was a time I dreamt of it. Plans postponed till I find a roof over my head and a safe job.

DOLLY: Good. We were not properly introduced that day, so let me. I'm Rajalakshmi Iyer but Dolly to everyone. My husband was in the army—retired now. I teach in the girls' public school next to Anjana's house. English elocution. For want of anything better to do. And our house is miles away from the school. So in between classes, I prefer to hang around in Anjana's house. Much nicer than the dreary staff room.

PRABHAKAR: You are obviously very close friends?

DOLLY: Very. She's a darling. Actually she used to spend her whole day idling at home. The idle rich housewife! I introduced her to the director of the Karunashraya, Kishore Rao. Now you have to drag her away from there.

PRABHAKAR: Karunashraya. Yes, that was mentioned that day. What is it?

DOLLY: A hospice. For cancer patients beyond hope. It was started by a dear friend, Kishore.

PRABHAKAR: And Anjana helps out there?

DOLLY: Virtually runs the show now.

PRABHAKAR: And her son? He is a guitar player?

DOLLY (*not interested*): I gather he's very good at the veena. But he plays the guitar. As a rebellion.

PRABHAKAR: Rebellion? Against whom?

DOLLY: His parents.

PRABHAKAR (*astounded*): While he lives with them? While they look after him?

DOLLY: I saw you were immersed in some book. What're you reading?

PRABHAKAR (*blushing as though caught red-handed*): Nothing really.

DOLLY: It's a secret?

PRABHAKAR: No, no, no. But I haven't started reading it. I just bought it the other day.

DOLLY: Tell me about it. I want to know more about you.

PRABHAKAR (*pulls the book out of his briefcase*): 'A Gentleman's Book of Etiquette.' Tells you all about—you know, if someone says 'How do you do' to you, don't say 'I am fine'. The correct reply is, 'How do you do'.

(*They laugh.*)

I learnt that this morning, now, sitting here.

DOLLY: Excellent. That's what I liked about you. Intuitively. That's why I asked you to come here this morning. A simple word from me was enough to get you started.

(*He is unsure of what she means.*)

That's what I like. You're an intelligent, well-read, energetic young man. You should treat the whole brave new world as a challenge, instead of creeping into the Padabidri house for a secret meeting, in search of a job.

PRABHAKAR: I could've been rotting in Mundgod. I'm fortunate to be in Bengalu—Bangalore. That's what I care about. This itself is release. The city air, however polluted, is an oxygen chamber, after the suffocation of a small town.

(*The bearer comes to them.*)

What'll you have?

DOLLY: Nothing, thanks.

PRABHAKAR: Nothing? Cappuccino, latté, espresso?
(*Dolly shakes her head.*)

> I'll have a cappuccino.

(*The bearer leaves.*)

> I learnt all these names only the other day. Until I came here, I only knew one brand, 'Coffee'.

DOLLY (*smiles*): You've passed all my tests with flying colours. So let me get to the point. Would you go to Singapore if you were offered a job?

PRABHAKAR (*flabbergasted*): You must be joking!

DOLLY: No, I'm not. Wipro has an office in Singapore. Will you accept a posting there?

PRABHAKAR: Please. Please. Don't make such cruel jokes. Wipro!

DOLLY: Azim Premji is a close friend. I was in college with his wife Yasmeen. At Xavier's.

PRABHAKAR: I daren't even dream of that world. Wipro! It scares me even to think of it. It's—it's listed on the Nasdaq!

DOLLY: And when I first met them, they were just plain ordinary people like you.

PRABHAKAR: I'm sorry. I just cannot grasp what you're suggesting.

DOLLY: Let me explain. The other day my husband and I had dinner with Azim and Yasmeen. And he was saying they were looking for a good regional manager for their Singapore office. But they want to fill it without any fanfare. They've their reasons for not advertising the post.

(*The coffee arrives. But he doesn't even look at it.*)

PRABHAKAR: But, Dolly, Mrs Iyer—

DOLLY (*laughs*): Dolly's fine. Go on.

PRABHAKAR: Wipro! It is one of India's largest .... Huge. Enormous. Azim Premji's up there! Will they even look at me? And why should they?

DOLLY: Are you going to listen to me? Or are you going to continue repeating yourself?

PRABHAKAR: Sorry. Sorry. But don't you see—

DOLLY: Look, I didn't ask them. He brought up the subject and asked me to suggest a good person. I've had a word with Azim since I met you. He is agreeable. There's only one proviso—

PRABHAKAR: What?

DOLLY: You've to leave for Singapore almost instantly. Right away. Can you? That's why I had to talk to you first before suggesting your name to them.

PRABHAKAR (*guarded*): How instantly?

DOLLY: Let's say you should've been there yesterday. Look, they've no shortage of people vying to get into the firm. They'll have a rioting mob there if the news leaks out. It's top secret. Don't even mention it to anyone. Or go to the Internet. Do you have to serve notice to your present bosses if you want to leave?

PRABHAKAR: I'm supposed to give them an advance notice of two months. Or pay two months' salary as penalty.

DOLLY: Good. Just pay the penalty and resign. Your monthly salary in Singapore'll be more than what you'll probably get in six months here. You'll be given residential quarters. And a car for your own use. Can you drive?

PRABHAKAR: Yes.

DOLLY: Good. Hand in your resignation tomorrow and get a move on.

PRABHAKAR: Tomorrow!

DOLLY: As soon as possible then. Look, try to understand the situation. You can't tell Wipro that you'll resign your present job only after getting their appointment letter. Things don't work that way. Ask your boss—did he have a formal appointment before he walked into the Padabidri camp? That's not how things are done in the modern business world. You've to prove you're interested in the post!

PRABHAKAP: I understand that. I understand that. But I've just managed to get my job. They've actually given me a probation in spite
of the rumpus caused by my boss. They've promised to confirm
me. What I always dreamt of. It's not so easy to walk off from it.
And my daughter's got into a good English-medium school—

DOLLY: It's up to you, of course. But you must learn to think afresh, see
it in its totality. This offer's there today. It certainly won't be there
tomorrow. Besides, wake up, Prabhakar! The era in which you
were expected to spend your entire lifetime serving a single firm
is gone. In this age of globalization you must move quickly, from
job to job and upwards. If you get this job, what are you going
to do with your wife and child? Are you going to leave them on
their own in Bangalore? You have to start thinking about that.

PRABHAKAR: I know. I know.

DOLLY: If you ask me, send them back to Mundgod to your par-
ents—or her parents. It's a question of only a couple of months.
Probably less. Then they'll in any case need to move to Singapore.
Bangalore isn't a safe place for a woman on her own with a child.
(*Long silence.*)

Look, you don't have to agree. If you think it's an unnecessary
risk, please don't go ahead. I don't want to arm-twist you.

PRABHAKAR: Do I have a choice?

DOLLY: Splendid. Buy some good new clothes—a well-cut suit or
two—and arrange monies for your initial expenses. I shall get
the interview fixed at the soonest. You know the Electronic City?

PRABHAKAR: I do.

DOLLY: You'll have to go there for the interview.

PRABHAKAR: Okay.   ᵒ

DOLLY: The first interview is a mere formality. Just for the record.
Someone from the Human Resource Development will see you.
Azim may ask you to meet him at his house later. You'll be in

Singapore before the end of the month. The real delay will be in getting the passport. You know the Passport Office! But they've someone to look after that. And, of course, they'll handle all the rest. Cheer up!

PRABHAKAR: How can I thank you enough, Dolly?

DOLLY: I've been very lucky in the friends I have. It's a question of spreading the luck around. So good luck!
(*She gets up, waves him a goodbye and leaves.*)

PRABHAKAR (*smiles*): Singapore, here I come!
(*He drinks the coffee in a single gulp.*)

Scene Six

Anjana's house. Anjana on the mobile. Frantic.

ANJANA: I was about to step into the shower when the phone rings and there's a call—from 'the other house where Vimala is employed', if you please—That's it. That's just it. I had no idea until that moment that Vimala had another job—a parallel one—in 'another house', with another family. And apparently there's an old woman there—the grandmother of the family and the commotion was all about how Vimala had stolen the grandmother's gold necklace—worth about three lakhs—a genuine gold necklace. And the mistress of the house was on the phone saying she'd taken Vimala to the Tilaknagar police station—Some Saroja Kunigal. They were both screaming their heads off. Vimala and her, grabbing the telephone from each other's hands, cursing each other, accusing each other of lying. I called Mr Infant instantly—Yes, yes, Mr Infant, the Deputy Inspector General of Police—Please, I *know* one shouldn't call the DIG of Bangalore simply because one's cook's in trouble, but what else was I to do? You couldn't be contacted for more than half an hour and you've strictly forbidden me to call your office for domestic problems. Anyway, I called Mr Infant .... What's the point of having friends in high places if you can't bother them? I didn't know where Kunaal was—So I rushed to the Tilaknagar police station. And I was there for two hours. Oh my goodness! The sub-inspector and Mrs Kunigal, Vimala, FIR, complaint—such shouting and screaming and recriminations. It was chaos. Then they said Vimala had to be there till the Inspector turned up. So I've come home. But I've said I'll be back with a lawyer and they can't do this to an innocent woman without evidence and what not. (*Pause.*) But on the way home I've been wondering. I mean I feel sorry for Vimala but couldn't there be some truth in the accusation. Who knows—recently we've been losing things in the house. Small objects, cash left on the table. Things have been disappearing, from the guest room. I had mentioned it to you—He's not home. Probably—You know he never tells where he's going to be. (*Suddenly exasperated*) Look, here I am, ringing you for advice in the midst of a domestic crisis. And you want to talk of Kunaal's activities—Yes, yes, we have to worry about him. But at the moment I have more immediate household headaches. Do you mind?

Scene Seven

Prabhakar's apartment. A tiny room now littered with metal trunks, old-fashioned holdalls, and cardboard boxes. His wife Sumitra is sitting on her haunches, weeping openly while packing a box.

PRABHAKAR: Where's the fourth box? Ah! Yes. What's this, Sumitra? Why are you being so silly? It's a question of only a month. Then we'll all be together in Singapore.

SUMITRA: I don't want to go to Singapore. I was so happy when you got a job here. Our own house. Our own life. No parents or parents-in-law to breathe down our necks. No interfering relatives. We were so happy. What more do you want?

PRABHAKAR: No, Sumitra. I'm rotting in this place. I must thank Dolly for making me realize I'm wasted here. I deserve a better job. I can't go on forever with this grind. And you deserve something much better. I'll see to it that you get the best in the world. I shall make you a queen.

SUMITRA: I don't want to go back. Why can't I just stay on here? Vishoo and I could join you in Singapore when you've settled down there. I just hate the thought of going back to that cesspit.

(Prabhakar has in the meantime dialed a number on the mobile.)

PRABHAKAR: Oh, you're there? Good. Please, will you please talk to her yourself?

(*Hands over the mobile to Sumitra.*)

Here. It's Dolly.

SUMITRA: I don't want to talk to her.

PRABHAKAR: Please, dear. She's only trying to help us.

SUMITRA (*into the mobile*): Hello—Yes, yes. I know—I know you mean well. And my husband says the same thing. But the thought of going back to that filthy place—I hate it! We were so happy here—I believe you. But Vishoo's got admission in a good school here. Back home there are no English-medium schools. And she'll miss a whole year—Is that so? They will? I believe you. Of course I do. Who else's there to guide us?—I know you've been running around for our sake—All right. Thank you so much. I'll be brave. Yes.

(*Returns the mobile to Prabhakar.*)

PRABHAKAR (*into the mobile*): Thanks, Dolly. I can't tell you how much I appreciate what you're doing for us.

(*Switching off the phone*) I hope that's convinced you. Such a good person. Taking all this trouble. For what? Look, there's no question of rethinking the decision now. I have resigned from my job. We've taken back the advance on rent. Things are happening, darling. What're you shedding tears for? Wipro is a dream company. People would kill to get a job there. The moment we get their letter, wheels'll go into motion. They've a separate department that looks after passports, work permits, visas—We don't have to do a thing. Not everyone gets such a break!

SUMITRA: I hate her. I don't know in which past birth I harmed her, that she should come back again as my tormentor.

Scene Eight

The police station. The Inspector is sitting behind a table. Facing him sit Vimala, Kunaal, and Mrs Saroja Kunigal, a woman of about forty-five, who is fuming.

INSPECTOR: Well, Vimala Thimmegowda, this Mrs Saroja Kunigal has filed a complaint against you. She says that you have unlawfully—

SAROJA: I thought so too, Sir—that *that* was her name. It isn't. Her real name is Vimala Mary Amaldas.

VIMALA: Don't believe her, Sir.

SAROJA: Two days ago, I went to Kamraj Road and met her parents. They're Christians. From Velankanni, who've moved to Bengaluru. Her name is Vimala Mary Amaldas. Her husband's also a Christian. The parents say they spent thirty-five thousand rupees on her wedding and, within six months, she'd dumped her husband.

VIMALA: She's talking nonsense.

SAROJA: I have their address here with me. Here.

INSPECTOR: I'll ask for it if I need it, thanks. Just recount the incidents quickly, please.

SAROJA: She's been working in our house for the past six months.

KUNAAL: Six months! Mummy had no idea at all.

VIMALA: Not six. I'd told Amma but she was of course lost in her own work. She's a busy person.

SAROJA: Don't believe a word of hers. I know she never told your mother she was working for us. She insisted it had to be kept quiet.

INSPECTOR: And you agreed? Didn't you ask for a reference?

SAROJA: We knew she was working in their house. That was reference enough for me. I desperately needed someone to look after my mother. So I accepted. I shouldn't have, of course. I know that now. But she seemed so nice.

INSPECTOR: So you didn't inform her mistress that you were going to employ her.

SAROJA: No. To be honest, I didn't. No.

INSPECTOR: You kept it a secret?

SAROJA: There was nothing to be secretive about. She went to their house to start cooking at eight-thirty in the morning. She agreed to come to our house an hour earlier and finish her duties within the hour. She didn't want to mix up the two jobs. It made sense.

INSPECTOR (*to Kunaal*): Have you ever lost anything in your house?

KUNAAL: No, never. She's been with us for over eight years and we haven't missed a single rupee.

INSPECTOR: No one pinches a rupee. (*Laughs at his own witticism.*) All right.

Go on, Madam.

SAROJA: My mother is eighty-eight. All this woman had to do was to come at seven-thirty, clean up the room, and bathe Mother. Pile up her used clothes for washing. That's all. It took less than an hour and I must admit she was good. She charmed my mother off her feet. Mother adored her.

VIMALA: You see, Kunaal. You do a job well and that's held against you.

INSPECTOR: Please don't interrupt.

SAROJA: My mother had a thick gold chain. A family heirloom. Would easily fetch three-and-a-half lakhs today. She normally took it off and left it on her pillow while she bathed. That was the routine. All these months, things have been going on smoothly. Two days ago Mother comes back from the bath and the chain isn't there! By the time she looks for it, this woman had dressed her up hurriedly and fled, saying she was getting late. I was upstairs doing my daily pooja and it was some time before I heard Mother calling out. I ran down and knew immediately what had happened. I called the driver and chased her in our car. But by that time she was already in front of their house (*points to Kunaal*), chatting with her boyfriend. I forced her back into our car, but of course the boyfriend fled. In his autorickshaw. We should've grabbed him—

VIMALA: Please don't use such foul words. Boyfriend! He isn't a boyfriend—he's my first cousin from the village.

SAROJA: A lover, more likely.

VIMALA (*flares up*): Please mind your words. If it was anywhere else I would have—

INSPECTOR: Please, Madam, please. Let's not have a public fight here.

SAROJA: Well, whatever he is, he's not her husband, that's for certain. She must have called him on the mobile. Or perhaps it was all planned in advance. The moment he saw our car, he scooted off and she tried to disappear into their house. But I got hold of her and dragged her back and we searched her. Of course the chain had vanished. No guesses on where it had gone.

VIMALA: Please don't make these vile accusations. He's from our village. A good boy. Like a brother to me. You ladies who're educated, you can only think of dirty things the moment you see a single woman.

SAROJA: Single? You? Ha. Who are you trying to fool? I haven't been sitting idle at home since that day you know. I've been investigating every bit of information about her. I've met her parents. She hasn't visited them in years. And now she's settled down with this auto-driver. I can give you his address.

INSPECTOR: We've him under surveillance, please don't worry. We've had his room searched.

SAROJA: They won't keep it at home. More likely they've sold it by now. You should—

INSPECTOR: It's not easy to sell a gold chain worth three-and-a-half lakhs.

VIMALA: Why should I leave my stuff in his room, Sir? I've nothing to do with him.

INSPECTOR: He had two trunks full of saris and women's clothes. When we asked him, he said he'd no idea who they belonged to or how they got there. He claimed he merely used the room to sleep at night.

VIMALA: If he doesn't know, how would I?

SAROJA: Now they have this loot—three-and-a-half lakhs—why should they claim those saris? They can just romp around—

VIMALA: Disgusting lies, Sir. All lies.

SAROJA: Don't think I'll let you get away. If I don't get that chain back I shall wipe the floor with you and your—your—You bitch!

INSPECTOR: Now now, Madam. No foul language. (*To Vimala*) Where do you live?

VIMALA: In Uttarahalli.

INSPECTOR (*looks at his file*): But the address you've given to the Padabidri family is quite different. It says Kadreguppe here.

VIMALA: Oh, that was when I'd just started working in their house. More than eight years ago, wasn't it? That was when my father was alive. I lived with my parents—

SAROJA: Why're you killing off your parents, wretch? They're still alive—hale and hearty. I met them only two days ago. (*To the Inspector*) Can't you see how she's lying!

INSPECTOR: We'll look into that. (*To Vimala*) I'm sending a head constable from our crime staff with you. There'll be a lady constable with him. Show them your house. We have to verify your details.

VIMALA: All right.

KUNAAL: I've got my car. I'll take them.

INSPECTOR (*calls*): Muniraju!
(*A constable appears and gives a half-hearted salute.*)

Check her details. (*To Saroja*) Would you like to go along?

SAROJA: What for? I know her details. She doesn't live in Uttarahalli. She's leading you up the garden path.

INSPECTOR: The head constable'll look into all that. And submit a report. We'll go on from there.
(*Kunaal and Vimala prepare to leave accompanied by the constable and the lady constable. Saroja follows them.*)

SAROJA: Be warned. She's a liar—a confirmed crook. She won't be easy to nail down. But I won't let her go. Let her watch out.
(*They all exit. The lighting changes and a spotlight picks up Kunaal as he speaks on the mobile.*)

KUNAAL: And so the four of us started in my car—me, Vimala, and the two constables. Actually, I was very annoyed with that Saroja woman. She'd continued to insult Vimala even when the Police were promising a proper investigation. I knew Vimala wasn't that kind of a woman—After all, we'd known her for more than eight years.

So we go to some new residential extension in Uttarahalli. I wish you were there, Nandita. It simply wasn't the Bangalore we know. No sign of any modern civic amenities there. An absolute nightmare from which there was no way of waking up. Of course the road had no pavement. In fact, there was no solid ground anywhere to step on—only potholes. Dirt, plastic bags, piles of garbage on which dogs were tearing at blood-sodden bits of menstrual rags. No way could you drive a car through. Stones heaped right in the middle of the road. And in one place, water poured out torrentially, seeming to gush out from the netherworld. And a regular washing ghat had sprung up right there—women washing clothes, pots, and pans by the roadside. And the houses! Oh god! They were like the cardboard containers in my father's warehouse—piled pell-mell almost on top of one another. And in the middle of all this chaos was a pink temple and beside it a livid green mosque. I somehow managed to navigate the car through this mess. There was a peepal tree and around it, a platform. It must have been the meeting place for the panchayat when this area was an independent village. A vestige from its independent past. The tree was intact and I could park next to it.

We got down and followed Vimala through the scrambled streets and reached a house in a remote corner. She took us to its outhouse which was facing away, almost in a sulk.

(*The lights come on the stage and Vimala and the constables join Kunaal.*)

VIMALA: That one in the backyard—that's my house. (*She goes to it and calls out.*) Sister-in-law, sister-in-law—

(*No reply. The constable goes to the house. The lady constable hangs around totally unconcerned.*)

Sister-in-law—

CONSTABLE: It looks empty.

VIMALA: No, no, the kitchen window is open.
(*Goes and knocks on the window shutter. A woman peers out. Looks at everyone without any expression and disappears.*)

Sister-in-law—

CONSTABLE (*loudly*): Listen, lady of the house, will you please come out?
(*The woman comes out of the front door.*)

WOMAN: What do you want?

CONSTABLE (*pointing to Vimala*): Do you know this lady?

WOMAN: The man of the house isn't in.

CONSTABLE: Do you know this lady?

WOMAN: Yes, I do. But we haven't seen her in the last six months.

VIMALA: Why do you say that, Sister-in-law? Don't I live here?
(*The woman gives a blank look.*)

CONSTABLE: Does she live with you in this house?

WOMAN: The man of the house isn't in. You ask him when he comes back.
(*Disappears into the house and shuts the door behind her.*)

VIMALA: That's my sister-in-law. My elder brother's wife. I live with them.
(*Knocks on the door calling out to the woman. When at last the door opens Vimala slips in. After waiting for either of them to re-emerge the constable makes a sign to the lady constable who goes into the house. The door remains open this time. The constable makes some notes. Suddenly the woman comes out.*)

WOMAN: Yes, she's my sister-in-law. She lives here.

CONSTABLE: But you said you hadn't seen her in six months.

WOMAN: Did I? I don't think so.

CONSTABLE: You said clearly you hadn't seen her for six months.

WOMAN: You ask the man of the house when he comes back.

CONSTABLE: I see that, apart from the bathroom, your house has a kitchen and an extra room. Do all three of you live in this space?

WOMAN: I've two children. They've gone to school. They live here too. (*Goes to the back of the house.*)

VIMALA: I sleep in the kitchen—with the children.

CONSTABLE: Can you all fit in?

VIMALA: Don't have a choice.

CONSTABLE: If you live here, you must have your things here—your saris, trunks, bags—something?

VIMALA: I've three saris and blouses. They were washed today. (*The constable looks around for some sign of the saris on the line.*)

Not here. There's no place here. I wash my clothes at Kunaal's place and dry them in their yard.

CONSTABLE: And what about other things? A trunk or a holdall to keep your stuff? Towels.

VIMALA (*laughing out*): My god! I don't have so much property.

CONSTABLE: I want to talk to your sister-in-law. Call her.

VIMALA: Sister-in-law—Sister-in-law— (*No response. Vimala pretends to search for her.*)

Not here. Probably gone shopping.

CONSTABLE: Without telling us?

VIMALA: Ayyo, but you aren't here to question her, are you? The poor thing has enough problems of her own. You can ask me anything. I'll explain.

CONSTABLE (*to Kunaal*): Shall we go?

VIMALA (*helpfully*): She may come back soon. If you're willing to wait—

(*The constable ignores her remarks and moves off accompanied by Kunaal and the lady constable. Vimala goes into the house and shuts the door.*)

KUNAAL: Is that all? Aren't you going to arrest her or do something?

CONSTABLE: Arrest her? What for? What's the point? (*Laughs.*) Our prisons have no spare capacity, Sir. Bengaluru's bursting with women like her. Where they live, how they live, how they move around—it's all a mystery. Impossible to pin them down. Like scorpions, you know. They only have to see a slab of stone and they'll crawl under it and set up house. Drop us near an auto stand, Sir. We'll go back on our own. Thanks.

(*The constables move off. Kunaal speaks into the mobile.*)

KUNAAL: I was flabbergasted, Nandita. Absolutely stunned. She's been with us for nearly eight years—and we've been saying oh such a nice woman, so reliable. And you know, every sentence she uttered to the police and to me was a lie. A bright, white, brazen lie. And she knew that I knew and the police knew that she was fibbing. And what courage! What invention! She was leading us on, she was creating a story from one minute to another. I tell you. She's my heroine. I've never seen such—such—what's the word—creativity! How could we've missed her brilliance!

(*Switches off the phone. And talks to himself.*)

She's simply wonderful. I wish she was my girlfriend. I think— I've fallen in love with her. What a woman! A true heroine!

Act Two

Scene One

The house of Shankara, Muttu's brother, in Karimangala town. As the lights come on, we see women and girls dressed in finery, participating in the coming-of-age rites for Kalpana, Muttu's daughter. She is aged about twelve and is seated on a plank decorated with alpanas. She has turmeric markings on her cheeks, and has oil poured down the parting in her hair. Then the women take their turns at circling a fistful of puffed rice in front of her. A girl sings a Tamil ritual song.

Shankara and Muttu's husband, Ravi, are sitting in a corner of the room. They are both wearing bright-coloured bush shirts and trousers. They are slightly drunk. The other men are in the outer room and cannot be seen.

MUTTU'S MOTHER: Come, Shankara. Now the girl's uncle has to pick her up and place her back on the plank. Come.

(*Shankara doesn't move. He continues to ignore her, obviously sulking.*)

Come on. Hurry.

(*There is no reply. The mother looks anxiously at Muttu. Muttu comes to Shankara.*)

MUTTU: Come, Brother. Come and pick up Kalpana.

SHANKARA: No, I won't come. I won't pick her up. What's she to me? What am I to you? Nothing. No relation. Don't you know that?

MOTHER: Don't say such inauspicious things, Son. Come.

SHANKARA (*snarling*): Why shouldn't I? Look at Kalpana. Decorated. Decked out like a bride. For what you're spending this evening you could've celebrated her whole wedding here. But if it was my daughter sitting there instead of Kalpana—if it was *my* daughter—would you have splurged like this?

WIFE: Please, let's not rake that up now. Not in front of all the relatives.

SHANKARA (*shouts*): You keep your mouth shut, will you? I'm telling them I've nothing to do with them. Don't poke your nose in all this.

(*The guests sense trouble and get restive. The women get up and draw their children closer.*)

MOTHER: Why do you say that, Shankara? Your daughter's my granddaughter too. She's as—

SHANKARA: Oh, is she now? So you've at long last remembered that, have you? And what have you done for these granddaughters, eh? They're rotting in this village. Do you ever think of them in Bengaluru? Do you even remember that they exist? What've you done for my daughters? Tell me.

MOTHER: What could I've done, Shankara? What did I have when I first went there? I was an unlettered widow and I was asked to get out of the house with Muttu, once my husband died. You know that. In the city, I could just about eke out a living by stitching and darning and mending for those Marwadis— mosquito curtains, bed sheets, window curtains—My legs're gone, as you can all see, just pedalling that sewing machine. Eight hours every day. Ten hours. And still there wasn't enough. I lost my legs stitching and sewing. Don't you know that?

SHANKARA: Enough, I tell you. Shut up. We've been through that song and dance routine hundreds of times. I was the older child and yet you didn't take me to Bengaluru. You didn't even bother about me later. It was Muttu, always Muttu—

MOTHER: Shiva, Shiva! How can you blame me? What choice did I have? You were a male child. You think your grandparents would have let me take you with me? They slung me out of the house with Muttu, saying they couldn't look after us. That we were a millstone. We lived like beggars, like roofless orphans, in that monster city. And when I found a job 'twas as a seamstress, chained to that sewing machine eight hours a day. Often even ten hours. What happiness did I ever see? It was all for you children—

SHANKARA: Don't you dare mention my children. How often did you spare a thought for us once you went there, eh? How often have you visited us?

MOTHER: Would your grandparents have let us into the house? I was the inauspicious woman who'd killed their son. But didn't your daughters come to the city? Didn't they stay with us in their holidays? We all loved having them. Didn't they enjoy the city?

SHANKARA: And came back hating this dump and our life here. You showed off nicely, I grant you that. Displayed how you and Muttu had flourished in the city, without us. How you'd prospered. And isn't that what you're here for now? To crow to our friends and relations—

MOTHER: God forbid. It was you who insisted we should have the rites here. You know that. You said we must have it here—

SHANKARA: Yes, so you would remember we're alive here. I had to practically drag you here. Would you've come otherwise? My wife's had two deliveries and you never offered to help.

MOTHER (*bursting into tears*): Why are you accusing me like this, Shankara? What help could I be? I can barely hobble. My legs swell if I so much as run around—

WIFE: Please, Husband, please, stop this now. All our relatives—

SHANKARA: I said shut up! Do you have any brains? Don't you understand if I tell you to shut up? One more word from you

and I'll thrash you in front of them. She treated us like pariahs—
She—she—
(*He virtually foams at his mouth.*)

Are you my mother? No, you're not. You are the mother of
Bengaluru Muttu. You've been no grandmother to my children.
Have you ever fondled them? Caressed them? You're a demon.
If we'd let you, you would even drink their blood. Aren't you
ashamed to call yourself my mother? You, you, I'll show you—
(*He attacks her. Starts beating her. Ravi, Muttu's husband, who has
so far been watching warily from a distance now jumps up and grabs
his hand.*)

RAVI: Are you in your senses, you drunken fool? If you're so sloshed,
go and sleep it off in a corner. Don't create a rumpus here.

SHANKARA: Ah! The great son-in-law himself. His royal self! Don't
you think I know who pays the fees of the English-medium
school? My daughters are condemned to Tamil schools, while
you stand pulling your locks in front of your mother-in—

RAVI: Hey! If you utter one more word I'll settle your hash right here.
Are you saying I can't pay for my own daughter?

SHANKARA: Go away! Your daughter—

RAVI: I warned you—
(*Attacks Shankara. They struggle. But Shankara is too drunk to fight
and Ravi beats him up. Pushes him into a corner from where his wife
helps him up and takes him away. There is pandemonium in the room.
The women gather their children and bundles and leave hurriedly.*)

WOMAN (*to the mother*): Ayyo, we've cooked food for thirty people.
They're all leaving. It'll all go waste. Please at least you have
some food.

MUTTU: Let's go, Mother. We've had enough of this home. Let's go
back to Bengaluru. I'm never going to step into this cursed town
again. I'm done with it. For ever. Come, Ma. Husband. Kalpana.
Let's go.

Scene Two

A new extension of the city, a virtually random arrangement of shape-less blocks of flats. Kunaal is sitting waiting patiently in a corner. Vimala arrives riding a scooter. She is surprised to see Kunaal.

VIMALA: Oh, Kunaal. What're you doing here?

KUNAAL: What else? Waiting for you.

VIMALA: How long have you been here? How did you get this address?

KUNAAL: I asked your sister-in-law.

VIMALA: She knew?

KUNAAL: Actually she didn't. I got it from Saroja Kunigal—you know, the lady who's accused you of stealing.

VIMALA (*suddenly rattled*): You mean—she had my address?

KUNAAL: Yes, and gave it to me without any fuss. She also added, 'Tell Vimala she can't escape me. I'll get her.'

VIMALA: Oh god! Such an evil woman.

KUNAAL: Is that your scooter?

VIMALA (*distracted*): What? Oh, this scooter? Where can I afford a scooter? It belongs to a cousin. He had to go away for a couple of days and has lent it to me.

KUNAAL: Why have you disappeared into thin air, Vimala? Mummy was waiting for you all day next day. The kitchen doesn't feel like one without you.

VIMALA: Who's been cooking?

KUNAAL: Mummy's got some temporary help. A Malayali woman.

VIMALA: Once the police have your address they start hounding you. They start visiting you. Every day. It's so embarrassing—attracts comments from the whole neighbourhood.

KUNAAL: My parents can help you there. You know they have friends in the police.

VIMALA: I don't want to bring you a bad name.

KUNAAL: No, you won't. Start coming to our house again from tomorrow.

(*An autorickshaw comes and stops nearby. A young man in the khaki uniform of a driver gets out, stands giving Kunaal a hostile stare, and then disappears round the corner.*)

KUNAAL: Will you come?

VIMALA: I don't know.

KUNAAL: Why not? We've no complaints against you. (*Laughs.*) Let me tell Mummy you're coming.

VIMALA (*horrified*): You aren't going to tell Amma you came and saw me here, are you? Please, don't. That'll only make matters worse.

KUNAAL: Why? I'm meeting you in broad daylight—in the open. Surely there's nothing wrong there.

VIMALA: There, that only means you don't understand. Please don't tell Amma you came to see me. She won't let me step into the house again.

KUNAAL: If she sends for you—

(*The young man comes out of the house and stands, glaring at them.*)

VIMALA: I'll give her a ring. I'll call this evening. No, tomorrow morning. But please, Kunaal, don't tell anyone about this house. I'm tired of running.

KUNAAL: All right. (*To the young man*) Hello, I am Kunaal. I'm sure Vimala has talked about me.
(*There is no reply.*)

VIMALA: He is my first cousin.

KUNAAL (*laughs*): Goodbye.
(*Goes off.*)

YOUNG MAN: They won't ever leave us alone. Will they?

VIMALA: Don't let him worry you. Come in.

Scene Three

The Reception Room of a Wipro office. Prabhakar is wearing a new suit, a bright new tie, and shoes.

PRABHAKAR: Good morning. My name is Prabhakar Telang. I've an appointment here for an interview.

RECEPTIONIST: And with whom would that interview be, Sir?

PRABHAKAR: Mr A.K. Gopalan.
(*The receptionist looks into her computer.*)

RECEPTIONIST: Are you sure, Sir? He's not in today. I doubt if he's in India since even his Personal Secretary's on leave.

PRABHAKAR (*taking out a letter from his pocket*): Here, I've a letter from Mrs Dolly—Mrs Rajalakshmi Iyer—confirming the interview.

RECEPTIONIST (*scans the computer*): But I'm sorry, there's no one of that name on our staff. I can't see that name anywhere. What department—

PRABHAKAR: No, no, Mrs Iyer is not a staff member of Wipro. I know that. She's a friend of Mr Azim Premji's. Mr Premji has confirmed to Mrs Iyer that Mr Gopalan will interview me today here. It's all there in the letter.

RECEPTIONIST: I'm sorry but this isn't Mr Premji's office.

PRABHAKAR: I know that. I know it's not his office. You see, there's a post for the Regional Manager in the Singapore office of Wipro.

RECEPTIONIST: I'm sorry, Sir. I know nothing about all those things. I'm only a receptionist here.

PRABHAKAR: I know. That's why I'm explaining it all to you. I've already been selected for the post of a Regional Manager in Singapore. What's on today is not an interview really. The selection's already been made. This is just a show to—

RECEPTIONIST: Sorry, Sir. If you were to meet Mr Gopalan, it should've been there on my schedule for today. And it isn't. And he isn't here. I can't help you.

PRABHAKAR (*slowly panicking*): Please don't say that. This is an important matter. A matter of life and death, you could say. I have resigned from my permanent job, paid the penalty of two months' salary, vacated my house, sent my family back to the village. Please, please, help me.

RECEPTIONIST: I'm doing my best to help you, Sir. That's what I'm here for. But Mr Gopalan isn't in office today and I've no idea when he'll be back. You don't even have a proper letter of appointment from this office. So what am I supposed to do?

PRABHAKAR: Look, it's not just a matter of my job. It's my whole life. I've taken a loan of seventy thousand. My entire future—everything hinges on this—this one meeting. Call it an interview, a meeting, anything. You understand what I'm saying, don't you? I've resigned a very nice job—
(*The receptionist presses a button and a security guard comes in silently. Prabhakar notices him and laughs.*)

No, no, I won't become hysterical and attack you, I promise you. But try to understand my plight. If Mr Gopalan isn't there, is there anyone else? There must be someone who looks after his work in his absence—perhaps Mr Premji himself? He knows Mrs Iyer. And I've borrowed—pawned our village land—for the preliminary expenditure. Wait. Wait. I know. I'll call Mrs Iyer. Will you talk to her?

(*The receptionist nods. Prabhakar presses a button on his mobile. Listens. Then with great relief speaks.*)

Oh Dolly! Thank goodness, you're there. What a relief! I was beginning to panic. I'm in the Electronic City. In the Wipro office—as planned—That's it. That's it—The interview hasn't taken place. The receptionist says she has no information. I'm baffled too. Can you speak to her? Please. (*To the receptionist*) Here. That's Mrs Iyer. Can you talk to her? Please.

RECEPTIONIST (*speaking on the mobile*): Yes, Ma'am. Tell me—Yes, yes. He's explained all that but I've no intimation from my office about it. None at all—He's not in the office—Please, Ma'am. Don't shout. I'm only doing my duty. I don't have to talk to you.

(*Hands back the mobile in exasperation to Prabhakar and waves him away. Goes back to her computer.*)

PRABHAKAR (*on the phone*): So, Dolly. What am I to do? All right. All right. I'll wait. (*To the receptionist*) She says she'll talk to Mr Premji and call me back.

RECEPTIONIST: You can wait here. No problem. (*When Prabhakar moves to a chair in the corner*) I hope you don't mind my saying so, Sir. But since I joined Wipro I've never heard of Mr Premji or his colleagues recommending anyone like this personally. It's entirely against the spirit of Wipro. People are selected on merit—

PRABHAKAR: But they've checked my merit and passed me.

RECEPTIONIST: Fine. Fine. Excuse me. I must get on with my work.

(*Prabhakar dials Dolly's number on the phone. But it's quite clear it's busy.*)

PRABHAKAR (*half to himself*): It's a nightmare! Seventy thousand—the village land—and then—

Scene Four

The garden outside Anjana's house. Anjana is trimming the hedge but it is clear her mind is not on the job. She is visibly upset. A mobile starts ringing inside the house and keeps on ringing. Muttu picks it up and comes rushing out.

MUTTU: Amma, Amma—Amma, your phone.
(*Anjana hurriedly wipes her tears.*)

ANJANA (*takes the phone*): Who's it? Oh, Vimala—Where are you? And when are you coming?—What?—Oh please don't tell me that. You can't do that to us! When are you coming back?— Ohho! All right. Come back as soon as possible.
(*She has been sniffing while talking on the phone. So ...*)

Nothing, nothing. Just a bad cold.
(*Switches off the phone and calls.*)

Muttu—
(*Muttu is right behind her near the door, having come to a sudden halt as soon as Vimala's name was mentioned.*)

MUTTU: Amma—

ANJANA: That was Vimala. She says she can't come back for another week. Some problem—has to go to her village. What're we going to do if she goes off like that? And Karunashraya is chock-a-block this week. They need every hand desperately. I can't let the nurses down at the last minute. We'll have to ask the hired cook—what's her name—if she can come for another week. Has she arrived?

MUTTU: Shalini rang earlier. When you were near the gate. Her child is sick. She won't be coming for the next two or three days, she says.

ANJANA: Oh dear! What then? Restaurant food for a week? I hate the thought.

MUTTU (*softly*): Amma—

ANJANA: Yes—

MUTTU: I can cook.

ANJANA: You can? And you didn't mention it all these days?

MUTTU: Vimala told me not to mention it. 'Just stick to your job,' she said.

ANJANA: Can you then handle the kitchen till she comes back? Bless you. You know Mr Padabidri's rarely home. And Kunaal loves eating out—UB City, Mainland China. It's just me. And of course there's Kunaal's grandma, for the next couple of weeks. But she handles her own food. You know that. Just basic food will do for me.

MUTTU: Yes, I do, Amma. And, Amma, I'm a Mudaliar by caste so—

ANJANA: Oh, for goodness sake, I'm not interested in your caste. Can you cook a decent meal? Rice and lentils?

MUTTU: Yes, I can, Amma.

ANJANA: Good. That's all that matters. Just whip up something for me then. Anything. With whatever's there in the kitchen.
(*Muttu doesn't move.*)

Go on. If you need any help, call me.

MUTTU (*in a low voice*): Amma, we've run out of cooking gas.

ANJANA: No gas? Nonsense. We have four cylinders.

MUTTU: There are only two in the house. And they're both empty.

ANJANA: I can't believe it. There should be four. Come. Let me see. (*Starts to go in.*)

MUTTU: Vimala has lent the other two to Professor Menon's family.

ANJANA: Who? Who's this Professor Menon?

MUTTU: Our neighbours. Recent arrivals. Their gas connection hasn't been sanctioned yet. So they've borrowed two of our cylinders. They've promised her they'll return them the moment—

ANJANA (*incredulous*): Vimala's given them two of our cylinders without telling me? I can't believe it.
(*No reply.*)

   Does she take money from them for the cylinders?

MUTTU: I don't know, Amma.

ANJANA: Since when's this been going on?

MUTTU: I don't know, Amma. That family moved into our neighbourhood some four months ago. We've only had two cylinders since then.

ANJANA: How terrible! Muttu, go to their house instantly and say we want the cylinders back. Right now.
(*Muttu doesn't move.*)

   Hurry. And don't accept any excuses. The shameless—

MUTTU: Amma, shall I also bring the microwave back?

ANJANA: The microwave? But our microwave—

MUTTU: The old one. Actually it wasn't working too well when they took it. But they've got it repaired and ours is giving a bit of trouble. And also the mixer—

ANJANA: Have they looted our entire kitchen? What else has she gifted to these Menons?

MUTTU: That's all. But they can keep the mixer. Our new one's very good.

ANJANA: And what about the fridge? Has she hired that out too?

MUTTU (*smiles*): No, Amma. It's too heavy.

ANJANA: Heavens! And all this under my very nose! I'd never have— Now go and tell them we want everything back. Even forks and spoons, if they've taken them. And this has been going on for four months!

(*Muttu is about to leave but stops.*)

MUTTU: Pardon me, Amma. Is there any bad news?

ANJANA: Bad news? Why?

MUTTU: Your eyes—

(*She indicates tears rolling down her cheeks with her two index fingers.*)

ANJANA (*wiping her cheeks*): Our rain tree. It's lying there looking so helpless. Like a baby. Just the trunk and the roots. I can't bear it.

(*Tears well up again and she wipes them. Muttu looks amused and goes in.*)

Scene Five

The race course. Anusuya and Sundara Rajan, poring over the racing notes.

ANUSUYA: Good. Let's go through it again so we're sure. Read that list again please.

SUNDARA RAJAN: Win and place for Number Three. Then Numbers Five, Eight, and Eleven for the second place?

ANUSUYA: Do you think Number Three is okay for a Win? Or should it be Eight, do you think? You know Eight won twice in Hyderabad. But somehow Three seems—why aren't you saying anything?

SUNDARA RAJAN: I won't say anything, Madam. You ask my opinion now and if the horse loses, you hold me responsible. I don't want anything to do with it.

ANUSUYA (*laughs*): Why would I grumble if your advice was anywhere near right? But look, look, look. I missed that completely. Flash Past. His father was Kubla Khan. And mother—what do you know? Queen Serenghetti. I would have missed him completely. They print these details in such small print. Queen Serenghetti. Do you know Serenghetti? My daughter Leena lives in Nairobi and she wrote to say that she went with her friends to the Serenghetti Park. I received her letter only yesterday and here it is! What a coincidence! Not a coincidence but a sign, surely! How much time do we have before the next race, Sundara Rajan?

SUNDARA RAJAN: Barely five minutes. Some two horses are to get into the boxes.

ANUSUYA: Then hurry up please! Bet on Flash Past. Twenty thousand for a Win.

SUNDARA RAJAN: Twenty thousand?

ANUSUYA: Yes, yes. Hurry, Number Four! Flash Past. Son of Queen Serenghetti. How could I miss him!

SUNDARA RAJAN: But look at the odds. That horse can't possibly win. Perhaps we can place a smaller—

ANUSUYA: Don't argue with me for god's sake. This is the last race of the season. Our last chance. Go. Run. Number Four. Flash Past. Twenty thousand.

SUNDARA RAJAN: Madam—

ANUSUYA (*fiercely*): I said go!
(*Sundara Rajan rushes to the booking window. She moves to the front of the gallery and leans on the balustrade. Sundara Rajan comes running and stands next to her.*)

ANUSUYA: Done? Good. Now!
(*The race begins and its progress is covered by the commentary on the soundtrack. They both watch eagerly and she gets wildly excited as the noise of the crowd swells.*)

ANUSUYA: Ayyayyo! Seven—Two's leading. Where the hell're our horses? They can't all be dead! Ah, there. There it is. Number Eight. Hurray. Keep it up. Eight!

SUNDARA RAJAN: Please, Madam. Be careful. Don't get too excited. Madam—

ANUSUYA (*screaming*): Ayyo! Look, it's Number Four coming up.
  Our Number Four. It's our Flash Past. Son of Queen Se—e—
  That's it. He's overtaken the rest. He's leading. That's it! Four!
  Four! Sundara Rajan—My fluke. He's won—He's won—Four!
  Hurrah—

(*Falls down in a faint.*)

SUNDARA RAJAN: Madam, Madam—

Scene Six

Anjana's living room. Dolly, sitting alone. A cement mixer which is roaring on the road outside goes suddenly silent. Dolly starts speaking on the mobile. At that exact moment the doorbell rings. Dolly ignores it, but while she is speaking, Muttu runs in from the kitchen and goes to attend to the door.

DOLLY: God, the racket outside! Can't hear a word. They're building the underpass. Thanks for the message. But, actually, tomorrow evening we've been invited to the Governor's Residence. A special concert. And do you know my husband forgot to tell me? What can you do with him?—It's Ayaan and Amaan, sons of Ustad Amjad Ali Khan.

(Muttu comes and stands signalling. Dolly, covering the mobile, gestures to ask her what she wants.)

MUTTU: Someone to see you, Madam.

DOLLY: Me? Here?

MUTTU: Says his name is Prabhakar Telang.

DOLLY: Oh? Ask him in.

(Muttu goes to the front door.)

I'll call you back. Someone to see me.

(Switches off the mobile and prepares to meet Prabhakar. Muttu comes in followed by Prabhakar and goes in.)

DOLLY: Oh, you! What're you doing here?

PRABHAKAR: I've come to see you. What else?

DOLLY: This isn't my house, you realize?

PRABHAKAR: I know. But I knew Anjana and Kunaal wouldn't be here now and you would. I'm without a job, you see. I spend all my time studying the movements of people.

DOLLY: Following someone around is called stalking. It's a legal offence.

PRABHAKAR: Why did you do it? Was it really necessary?

DOLLY: Was what necessary?

PRABHAKAR: That's great. You ask me. My wife's refusing to come back to Bangalore. She says what humiliation she's suffered will last her a lifetime. I'm penniless. Why did you do it?

DOLLY: You're right. Why do I do it? I keep asking that question to myself. Why do I want to run around and then get blamed in the end? I know some influential people; they could be of help; they're willing to help. But in the end I get the blame. My husband keeps asking me that question. I run around for months arranging everything and you don't show me the courtesy of waiting there for half an hour more.

PRABHAKAR: Where?

DOLLY: In the Wipro office. I rang after half an hour and you were gone. You threw a tantrum, the receptionist told me.

PRABHAKAR: And what was I to do sitting there? And for how long? Do you know how desperately I tried ringing you? And you were busy. Busy. I couldn't get through to you—

DOLLY (*flares up*): What else did you expect me to be if not busy? Talk of ingratitude. Of course, my mobile was busy. Because I was trying to get in touch with Azim Premji, to find out what'd gone wrong. You think he's so easy to contact? Fortunately he was in

Malaysia. At least I could talk to him. In the States it would have been midnight. And he got in touch with his office. He didn't know Gopalan was away. But he told Phillips. And insisted the arrangements had to go through.

PRABHAKAR (*incredulous*): He called the office? That day?

DOLLY: Yes, immediately, for my sake. And instructed Phillips to proceed as planned. That day. But where were *you*? You'd simply vanished.

PRABHAKAR: I was seriously contemplating suicide.

DOLLY: And didn't go ahead, I can see. Instead you've created the most embarrassing situation for me. Dreadful. I've never been in such a predicament before. I can't face my friends. I haven't seen Azim and Yasmeen since that day—and we used to meet every other day. And then you've the gall to ask me if that was necessary! You've the bloody cheek!

(*A long pause. Then*)

PRABHAKAR: Before I came in now, I was standing outside, for nearly ten minutes, wondering if I should enter. The concrete mixer was bellowing away, so I knew we wouldn't hear each other anyway. And I was fascinated by that mixer with its huge grotesque striped belly. And those bright yellow long-necked earth diggers and extractors with sharp claws and fangs. What are they here for? For me. So I could use these streets. Go over flyovers. Flow with the crowds. To give meaning to all this—this mess, this chaos. I keep asking myself: what keeps things working at all in this city? What drives these crowds? Hope. Ambition. Whatever. It's our version of the American Dream, which would've horrified my parents, but has brought me to Bangalore. It seemed poised to lead me on to Singapore. But no matter. Despite the lesson you've taught me, Dolly, I promise you, I shall pursue that dream. I shall be relentless in a—

(*Suddenly the concrete mixer erupts into action again outside, with a deafening roar. They can't hear each other. He shrugs his shoulders, laughs loudly, waves goodbye, and moves to the door. There he runs into Brigadier Iyer coming in, bows to him elaborately as though they were old friends, and walks out. Baffled, the brigadier turns to his wife to ask who that was. Dolly gestures that she hasn't a clue. They go out. The noise outside continues.)*

Scene Seven

Muttu's house in another part of Bangalore. Vimala arrives on a scooter. Calls out.

VIMALA: Muttu—Muttu—
(*Honks loudly. Muttu enters.*)

MUTTU: Oh, Vimala! How nice. Come in. Come in.

VIMALA: No time to come in. Let's talk here. How're you?

MUTTU: Okay. As usual.

VIMALA (*smiling*): Oh, better than usual, surely. You've got a promotion.

MUTTU (*confused*): What was I to do? Amma said you hadn't come or you weren't coming or something like that. Asked me to take charge till you came back. That's all.

VIMALA: And you got stuck for good. Very nice. I worked there for eight years. You've set yourself up for the next eight now.

MUTTU (*her eyes fill up*): No, I swear to you I didn't mean to steal your place. If you decide to come back today, say so and I'll happily go back to the cleaning and washing. I promise.

VIMALA: Is your mother in?

MUTTU: Yes. Busy with her stitching and sewing. As usual.

VIMALA: Can I say hello to her?

MUTTU: Of course. Mother, Vimala's here!

MOTHER (*from inside*): Why don't you ask her to come in? Sit down for a while?

VIMALA: Do you mind coming out? Please. I don't want to leave the scooter in the street. You can never be sure.
(*Muttu's mother hobbles out on her stick.*)

How are you, Gangamma?

MOTHER: What can I say? You know my legs. They're gone. All that—

MUTTU: I asked her to step in and sit for a while. But she won't.

VIMALA: Let's skip the formalities now. What I've come to tell you is, when I was in trouble your daughter grabbed my job. It was nicely done.

MUTTU: That's not true. I promise you—

VIMALA: Shut up! Who snitched to Amma about the gas cylinders? Those two cylinders were lying idle, and my only thought was to help the Menons, poor them. That's all. I didn't steal them for myself, did I? And yet you tattled to Amma—

MUTTU: No, no, listen, please. There was no gas in the house—

VIMALA (*almost fiercely*): Stop whining and listen to me. You swiped my job and saw to it that I would never get it back. (*To the mother*) Now let me give you a piece of news. Your son Shankara. He's in Bengaluru.

MUTTU: Really? Where?

MOTHER: How do you know my Shankara?

VIMALA: Don't you remember? You brought him to Amma's house to see Muttu. About her daughter's growing-up ceremony. I never forget a face. How else do you think I've survived in this city?

MOTHER (*already getting panic-stricken*): Shankara's here? Where's he?

VIMALA: Listen to me. A few days after that row he had with you and Muttu's husband in your village, he moved to this city. He's left his wife and daughters back home and bought himself an auto-rickshaw. He lives here.

MOTHER: Oh god! Why didn't he tell us?

VIMALA: Why would he? He hates you like poison. Get in touch with you? He hasn't let on to anyone here anything about himself. Where he's from. His name. Address. Nothing. I went to see my cousin at the auto stand and who should I see there but …? When I said, 'Aren't you Muttu's brother, Shankara?' he almost jumped out of his skin.

MUTTU: Where's he?

VIMALA: He shares a garage with some half-a-dozen young men—all auto drivers.

MOTHER: Ayyo, why does my son do things like that?

MUTTU: How's he?

VIMALA: That's what I came to tell you. He's in the hospital.

MUTTU and MOTHER: Hospital? What happened? Oh mother of mine—

VIMALA: Half a dozen boys in a room together. Can't you imagine the shenanigans? Drinks. Drugs. Street women. Apparently there was a fight the other day. They brought out their bicycle chains and knives. Now he is in the general ward of a hospital wrapped up in bandages. And the hospital won't keep him for long if he doesn't produce some cash. (*Pause.*) And in this entire city, only I know who he is.

MOTHER: Please, please, I must go and see him immediately. Right now.

MUTTU: Hold on, Mother. Let's at least find out the name of the hospital.

VIMALA: There you are, practical as usual. You've a permanent job now. You've eight years in which to find out where he is. If he lives that long. Bye—

(*Turns to go. The mother tries to stop her, but cannot catch up with her and collapses on the road. Muttu grabs hold of Vimala.*)

MUTTU: Please, Vimala. Please. Tell us where he is. You can't do this to us. Mother'll die of anxiety.

VIMALA: I don't give a damn. Enjoy your job. Let go of me!

Muttu: Vimala—please—

(*Vimala pushes Muttu aside, gets on the scooter, and drives off. Muttu runs to her mother and helps her up.*)

MUTTU: Don't believe her. I won't swallow a word she's saying. She's a liar. Always was.

MOTHER: No, no, she's telling the truth. I can feel it in my bones. My Shankara's in trouble, Muttu. We must find him. He's lying in some hospital! I know she's telling the truth—

MUTTU: All right, all right. I'll tell Husband. We'll look for him. Don't worry, Mother. Husband's bound to find him. Come in now.

(*Helps her up.*)

Scene Eight

Night. Bedroom in Anjana's house. Anusuya is resting and Kunaal is sitting by the bedside.

ANUSUYA: What's this band of yours, Kunu? And why are your parents so unhappy about it? You used to play the veena and so well too. We all thought you would grow up to be a great veena player.

KUNAAL: Will you come and listen to my band?

ANUSUYA: No, I won't, if you don't mind. I just can't come to all those places. But send me a cassette and I'll listen to it.

KUNAAL: No one makes cassettes any more, Grandma. And I haven't managed to get an album out yet.

ANUSUYA: Why not?

KUNAAL: The music companies want me to add something 'Indian' to my music. 'Add a flute,' they say, 'or some tabla. You know. Sitar, Indian culture. A few strains of veena. Then it'll have a market.'

ANUSUYA: But what's wrong with that? It is our music.

KUNAAL: It's not my music, Grandma.

ANUSUYA: But you were so good at the veena.

KUNAAL: I know. Papa and Mummy would've been happier—or let me say, less unhappy—if I'd continued with that. Veena is so prestigious!

ANUSUYA: But all those years of training—are they going to be wasted?

KUNAAL: No, no, they've proved most useful. My fingertips had got calloused thanks to the veena. They were in condition for the guitar.

ANUSUYA: I suppose I should leave it all to you. You know what it's about. But do you know where you get your talent from? Your mother. She was so gifted—a divine voice she had. Every time she sang, the women of my age in Dharwad would sigh and say, 'I wish I could have her as my daughter-in-law.'

KUNAAL: She did become your daughter-in-law.

ANUSUYA: To tell you the truth—I suppose I can tell you now—when she agreed to marry your father, it broke my heart. He has no art in him whatsoever. You get it all from her. I often wonder why she said yes to him. (*Kunaal is amused and laughs.*) Somehow, after marriage, she lost her gift. And I don't suppose he's even noticed.

KUNAAL: She hums—rarely. A nice voice. The problem with her is that she feels she must support Papa. I've a suspicion that deep down she doesn't at all mind my heavy metal band. But she stood behind Papa when they struggled in their youth. Now she must be at his side in their old age. The devoted Hindu wife.

ANUSUYA: You should've heard her sing—specially the compositions of Saint Purandara Dasa. The entire audience would be moved to tears.

KUNAAL (*excited*): That's it, Grandma. I consider myself an avatar of Purandara Dasa too. Truly. He composed his own songs. So do I. He broke away from traditional music. So have I. And he never played in the royal courts. He took to the streets. You told me that. And I don't play in the pompous concert halls either.

For me it's the clubs, garages, and pubs. I don't believe in God. But in a way, I suppose, music is my god.

ANUSUYA: That's all right then. If that's what you believe. You know Purandara Dasa searched for God all over the world. And then he didn't even know it when God came and stood, right in front of him. I thought all that was possible in earlier ages. Treta. Dwaapara. But I tell you, Kunu, when that Number Four, Flash Past, suddenly shot out and overtook the other horses, I—I—I suddenly had that vision. How can I describe it? At that moment I saw God. Vividly. For a moment He was there—for me. Real. I saw Him. Then I don't know if it was the Truth or just an illusion. I'm not that erudite. And perhaps that's why Flash Past lost at the last moment. If he'd won and I had collected all that cash, it wouldn't be a divine experience, would it? It would've been just a fluke, not a vision. God's not there to keep us company permanently. He shows Himself and is gone. And for me that was enough. God showed himself to me. (*Her eyes fill up with tears.*) What more could I ask for in this life?

(*She wipes her tears. He too is deeply moved by her words. They continue to sit in silence.*)

Scene Nine

The Padabidri living room. Dolly, alone, talking to someone on the mobile.

DOLLY: … And what your boyfriend told me simply amazed me.
(*Muttu enters.*)

Excuse me, just hold on.
(*Dolly lowers her mobile to listen to Muttu.*)

MUTTU: Madam, Amma called. The train left on time. But the traffic's so bad they're stuck on South End Circle. They may not be home for another fifteen minutes.

DOLLY (*eager to continue her phone conversation*): Thanks.

MUTTU: It was just like that here outside our house too, Madam. Noise, honking, petrol fumes. Thank god for the underpass. It's so peaceful now. Shall I make you some tea in the meanwhile?

DOLLY (*waving her away*): Not to worry. My husband will be here any moment.

MUTTU: It won't take a minute. Boiling hot and just one spoonful of sugar. I know.
(*She goes in. As she continues on the mobile, Dolly peers out of the window to make sure her husband hasn't arrived and continues.*)

DOLLY: No, no, it's no favour. I just happen to know some influential people. Two years in ballet and then Bharatanatyam—that's some training, Asha. You can't just throw all that away! I know the director of the Trinity Laban Dance School in London and he was asking me why they didn't get enough students from India. Despite all the facilities—No, money's no problem. That's the thing. There are scholarships. And bright girls like you must make use of them.

(*Brigadier Iyer enters and stands silently listening. She is so carried away by her own words she doesn't notice his arrival.*)

It's laughable that a dancer like you should be a dance teacher in a school. That's no better than being a drill teacher, is it? My advice is resign the job and get out. Launch out. Don't wait. You must leave immediately and go for an—

(*Notices her husband and switches off her mobile, half way through the sentence, and waits tensely for his next move. He glares, then goes up to her, and starts slapping her. She puts up with it as though she is used to it. In a low voice*)

Not here. Not here. Please.

(*Muttu steps in with her tray carrying a pot of tea. She pretends not to have seen what's been happening.*)

BRIGADIER (*in a flat voice to Dolly*): We had a flat tire. I've asked the car to be taken home directly once the puncture's repaired. Took a cab here. Let's go.

(*He goes out. Dolly turns to Muttu.*)

DOLLY: Tell Anjana I had to go back urgently. And here, if you're ever in need, just call me.

(*As she puts the mobile back into her handbag, she takes out a five hundred rupee note and gives it to Muttu who takes it without a thank you and tucks it in the sari-knot on her waist. Dolly leaves. Muttu's mobile rings. She speaks.*)

MUTTU: Oh god, Mother, I've told you a hundred times not to ring me here. Amma doesn't like it. Yes, yes, Husband's in touch with the police and they're looking for him. Bye. I must rush.

(*Switches it off. To herself in exasperation*)

As though we've nothing else to do. The brute. He'll get in touch if he needs to.

(*Anjana and Kunaal come in.*)

Dolly madam and her husband were here and said they had to go.

ANJANA: Yes, I saw them.

MUTTU: Some Mr Raykar called three times. Wanted your mobile number but I refused to give it to him. He's left his number.

(*Gives a piece of paper to Anjana. At the mention of Raykar, Kunaal becomes attentive.*)

And I've brought a woman to do the cleaning and ironing. She's a neighbour—

ANJANA (*transferring the number to her mobile*): Ask her to wait, please.

(*Muttu leaves. Anjana, almost to herself*)

Raykar? Some new admission?

KUNAAL: He's a pawnbroker. A moneylender.

ANJANA (*startled*): How do you know?

KUNAAL: I noticed that Grandma didn't mind using our car when she went on her social rounds. But never, when she went to the races. She didn't want to disturb your schedule, she said, and always hired a cab from the taxi company. So I probed a bit. It was quite routine for her to stop at Raykar's on the way to the races. So I went and met Raykar. Grandma's been borrowing money from him. Regularly.

ANJANA: You knew all along! And didn't let me know?

KUNAAL: I didn't see why I should if she didn't want to. I assured him the deal was safe and told him to carry on. I said not to disturb the arrangement until she was gone. (*Pause.*) Now she's gone and he's on the phone. She's borrowed close to two-and-a-half lakhs from him.

ANJANA (*horrified*): She has what? (*He shrugs.*) But two-and-a-half lakhs, Kunu!

KUNAAL: Did you never wonder where she got all the money to bet on the horses? Week after week?

ANJANA: But—but—this Raykar—he trusted her with that amount?

KUNAAL: She pawned her jewellery.

ANJANA : Oh my god! Kunu!

KUNAAL: What?

ANJANA: Her gold bangles and diamond earrings and pearl pendants— Two-and-a-half lakhs splurged on horses!

KUNAAL: Why not? Her son can afford it. Why shouldn't she indulge? If she'd asked for money, she would have been treated to long sermons by both of you. And I know how *that* feels. Actually I feel decimated that this method of conning Papa never occurred to me. I feel such a dunderhead. She's a true genius.

ANJANA: Don't you feel ashamed to say these things against your father? He would be heartbroken if he heard about his mother—

KUNAAL: Not for the first time, I'm sure.

ANJANA: Yes, he's made money. So what's wrong with that? Do you know how he's slogged for it—travelled all over the world— worked through the nights? And what gives you the right to run him down? I haven't seen you have qualms about spending his money.

KUNAAL: I know and I don't care. What amazes me is how you stick by him. Does it really matter to him what you or I do? Even Grandma says you've let your singing go to pot for his sake and he hasn't even noticed.

ANJANA (*astounded*): Did Grandma really say that?

KUNAAL: Something like that. She should know.

ANJANA: No, she doesn't. She is wrong. (*Pause.*) Very wrong.

KUNAAL (*turning away*): There you go. I knew—

ANJANA: No, no, that's one thing I won't let you blame your father for. She's wrong. All right. Since you've asked me, let me tell you—

KUNAAL: What?

(*Pause, as Anjana gathers courage to continue. Kunaal, impatiently*)

What?

ANJANA: You should probably know about it anyway. You're old enough now. You were not even two then. We'd just moved to Bangalore and were living in a chawl—two tiny rooms in a corner. And Papa worked. He travelled around day and night as an Operations Manager. He was making plenty of money. But he was never there when I wanted him. I don't blame him. I could feel myself slowly going crazy. And to keep myself sane, I used to sing out—loudly.

(*Pause.*)

One day there was a knock on the door. It was a young man who lived next door to us. A Bengali. He too was alone. No friends, no relations. I can't remember what he did. Some kind of a software job that kept him mostly at home. When he realized how welcome he was, he started coming regularly to our house. He would come. Laugh. Crack jokes. Play with you.

(*Pause.*)

He had a nice voice and we often sang together—mostly Hindi film songs. But also Rabindra Sangeet, which he taught me. Even the correct Bong pronunciation. With him around, time just flew.

(*Pause.*)

I woke up one day and he was gone. He had vacated his room and left. He had tacked a note for me on my door. It said, 'I don't

wish to be trapped into a relationship with a married woman.'
Trapped!

(*Pause.*)

I used to suffer from insomnia those days. Had a large caché of
sleeping pills. I ground some pills in milk and fed them to you. I
swallowed the rest. I then prayed to the gods, clasped you to me,
and went to sleep—never to wake up again.

(*Pause.*)

I don't know how long we were sleeping like that. No one
would've known for days if we'd died. But I suddenly opened
my eyes and sat up. Bright and wide-eyed. I was alive and so
were you. Death had cheated us both.

(*A very long pause. At last*)

I could never sing again after that. I'd lost my voice.

(*Pause.*)

KUNAAL: Why do you say that? I've heard you sing—or at least hum
in your bathroom—

ANJANA: I found it again, years later, in Karunashraya. One evening,
I was sitting with a patient—she'd only a couple hours to live—
and she said to me, 'Can you sing? Will you sing something
for me?' And I suddenly found myself singing. A composition of Purandara Dasa's. 'When you've been given human life,
and have a tongue, shouldn't you sing of Krishna?' The song
just poured out, on its own. (*Pause.*) And so did the tears. At
long last.

(*Pause.*)

But somehow singing never meant the same again.

KUNAAL: Have you ever told this to Papa?

ANJANA: No, but perhaps I should tell Grandma.

(*They laugh. A long pause.*)

KUNAAL (*with great difficulty*): I'm only asking because you mentioned him—but did you—were you in—Did you love that young man?

ANJANA (a*s though trying to sort out her memories*): I don't think so. If I had, do you think I would've reacted as I did?
(*Kunaal's face brightens.*)

KUNAAL: That's all right then. Nothing really happened!

ANJANA: I could have lost you!
(*Suddenly she hugs him. They stand still for a couple of minutes, holding on to each other, in a rare, tight embrace. Then Anjana moves back wiping her tears.*)

KUNAAL: You know what, I'm going to set those words of Purandara Dasa's to music. To *my* music. And then we'll have a proper show. We'll present you on stage: 'The Kunaal Padabidri Band presents Anjana Padabidri, the Singing Sensation …'

ANJANA: Spare me, please. Do what you like, but leave me alone. In any case, no one'll hear my voice in all the racket you make.
(*They both laugh. Anjana moves calling out to Muttu.*)

Muttu, this new cleaning woman—
(*She goes in. Kunaal sits, brooding. Then slowly he pulls out his mobile and speaks into it.*)

KUNAAL: Nandita, I've just realized something I'd never thought of before. I might not have been here at all now. I may never have existed, and yet the world would've continued to be, exactly as it is now. I mean. This world, this city, Bangalore, my friends, family, you—everything would have existed, but not me. I could be inside some black hole! I wouldn't be existing. What an utterly horrible thought! But if I didn't exist, whether the rest of the universe existed or not, *that* wouldn't have mattered in the least, would it?—
(*As he speaks, behind him, the stage fills with the characters of the play. They are not stiff now or frozen, and stand at ease listening to him. A*)

girl, presumably Nandita, comes and sits close to him, smiling at what he is saying. He puts aside his mobile, takes out his guitar from its case and starts strumming it as he continues to speak to her.)

That's going to be my new composition—yes—my paean to Bangalore that might never have existed. You know what's the first line? 'Big Bang Bangalore is a Big Black Hole!'

(Gentle laughter from the crowd. He starts humming a tune and trying it out on his guitar.)

(Fade out.)

About the Playwright

Girish Karnad, one of the finest playwrights, film-makers, and actors of our time, writes in Kannada and has translated his plays into English. Presenting a critical sense of history, myth, and time, his plays make a confluence between the past and the present.

Born in 1938, Karnad did his graduation from Karnatak University, Dharwad, in mathematics, and was a Rhodes Scholar, which took him to the University of Oxford where he received an MA in philosophy, politics, and economics. On his return to India in 1963, he joined Oxford University Press as an editor. In 1970, however, he left the Press to continue his writing. He was awarded the Homi Bhabha Fellowship the same year for studying pre-modern Indian theatre. The Fellowship enabled him to explore the potential of traditional conventions and techniques in dealing with contemporary themes; he came out with the play *Hayavadana*. The response was electric; the play pioneered a new movement in Indian theatre.

Former Director of Film and Television Institute of India, Pune, and Director of The Nehru Centre, London, Karnad was also Chairman of Sangeet Natak Akademi (National Academy of Music, Dance and Drama). During his tenure in the Akademi, he played a decisive role to save the ancient theatre form Kutiyattam from extinction. During 1987–8, he was at the University of Chicago as Visiting Professor and Fulbright-Playwright-in-Residence.

Karnad's plays have been directed and presented by eminent theatre directors like Ebrahim Alkazi, B.V. Karanth, Vijaya Mehta, and Satyadev Dubey. His *Naga-Mandala* was premiered in the US in 1993 by the Guthrie Theatre, Minneapolis, which then commissioned *The Fire and the Rain*. In 2002, the Haymarket Theatre, Leicester, UK, commissioned and premiered his *Bali, the Sacrifice*.

Karnad's *The Dreams of Tipu Sultan* was commissioned by the BBC Radio and broadcast in Britain on 15 August 1997 to celebrate the 50th anniversary of Indian independence. He wrote and presented the film *The Bhagavad Gita* as part of the series 'Art That Shook the World', for BBC Two in 2002. Actively involved in the visual media as actor, director, and script-writer, Karnad has directed films in Hindi and Kannada and acted for film-makers like Shyam Benegal, Nagesh Kukunoor, Satyajit Ray, Mrinal Sen, and Kabir Khan.

The International Theatre Centre of UNESCO, Paris, has declared Karnad World Theatre Ambassador of the International Theatre Institute, Paris. He has been honoured with the Padma Bhushan and was conferred the prestigious Jnanpith Award. Among the academic honours conferred on him is the degree of Doctor of Humane Letters, Honoris Causa by the University of Southern California, Los Angeles.

Girish Karnad lives in Bangalore.